Google SuperVote For 1

Google Images of a New World!

Michael Mathiesen

Copyright 2014 – by Michael Mathiesen

Table of Contents

Introduction
Chapter One: Google SuperVote
Chapter Two: So You Want To Run for President
Chapter Three: The Real Evolution
Chapter Four: The Corporation
Chapter Five: The Bylaws
Chapter Six: The Balance Sheet
Chapter Seven: National Ballot Measures
Chapter Eight: The Grass Roots
Chapter Nine: Can Government really make a profit?
Chapter Ten: Corporate Government– the ultimate IPO
Chapter Eleven: The First Internet Constitutional Convention.
About The Author:

Learn how these crazy ideas have evolved by reading some of my other books

<<<<< http://MichaelMathiesen.com >>>>>

AND Updates about this book ->

UsingGoogleSuperVote.com

Introduction

I became interested in real democracy in America when I was asked by President Nixon to join him and participate in the horror known as Viet Nam. It was this most perplexing moment in my life that made me realize there had to be a better way to conduct the affairs of what I, and many millions of other people all over the world considered to be the greatest country of all time. This book is a product of that life-long quest to make this country honor the promise of a Real Democracy given to the world.

Everyone I knew, millions of Americans, were protesting against this war. Yet, one man, Lyndon Johnson and then his successor Richard Nixon defied the will of the vast majority of American people and decided to have his little war despite public opinion, citing 'The Silent Majority'. According to Nixon's theory of Government, most people supported his psychopathic ideas by their silence. Until the invention of the Internet, we had no voice, so he could consider us a 'Silent Majority' and much of the evil in this world is perpetrated even today under this banner.

With Google Super-Vote and the rest of the Internet's wonderful technology the MAJORITY need not, nor can be silent any longer.

I also want my readers to remember the famous words uttered by President George W. Bush. When asked why he was taking our country into the War in Iraq, he said, "Because I'm the 'Decider'. So, this country was forced to live with the decisions made by this morally bankrupt and traitorous person. (Don't worry - I'll prove these charges later in this book.) The only question we should be asking ourselves at this point in time, is "HOW on EARTH did a so-called Democracy, the greatest country in the world devolve into a system of government that has ONE DECIDER who has now brought us to the level of a third world country?"

In this book, you will learn that in fact, we no longer have to live with only the decisions made by men like these. Because of the modern technology given to us, ironically by the same government, we are now fully capable to make our decisions in a common arena of debate, the testing of the best ideas, and then the final choice of the best ideas by using Google Super Vote and/or supporting Internet technology.

The 2nd American Revolution Starts NOW. But it's not a shooting Revolution. It's the Internet Revolution. It's what I call the transition from uncontrolled Capitalism to a very responsible new form of economic model I call 'Government Capitalism'.

The idea came to me while I was watching one of my favorite TV shows, American Idol. I like to watch the show because of all the talented people and the way that they use their audience to pick the season winner. The first year of the competition, it was Kelly Clarkson who won and I was a fan since the first time I heard her sing on the show. So, I was ecstatic when she won. I believed that I helped her win because I voted for her every time. Now, every time I see her appearing on TV or when listening to one of her records, I feel closer to her because I picked her from day one to win.

Then, through successive seasons of the show, I was in accordance with the winner, about 9 out of 10 times. This proved to me a concept that I later came to see as the 'Wisdom of the Crowd'. This is research that has been done over the last thirty or forty years by the American government. The CIA funded a 30 year study about how their own assessments of world situations compared to what the average citizen had come to realize. They studied over 3,000 citizens by sending them surveys. The American citizens were picked at random.

Amazingly, ONE HUNDRED PERCENT of the time, the study found, the average American citizen chose the final assessment of the world situation better than the CIA had done themselves. This was a shocking result to them, not to me, because the CIA has access to all the information, including the classified stuff that no one ever gets to see, except someone with the highest government security clearance. The average citizen always chose the best solution to the problem and this was based on their reading the news or watching it on TV and then putting it all together in their own ways.

In another study done by a major university, they asked several thousand people to guess the weight of an animal pictured on the

Internet. They could only see the size of the animal in relation to other objects like people standing nearby and trees and buildings nearby.

The average weight that was guessed was 1,179 pounds. The real weight of the animal was 1,178 pounds. They were off by an insignificant one pound. Remember, they had never been near the animal. They only saw a picture. The sum total of all their guesses and then turned into an AVERAGE was off by ONE POUND.

This is the 'Wisdom of the Crowd'. If you asked one or two people what the weight of this animal is, they would probably both be off by several hundred pounds. But, when you ask enough people, you get very close to the absolute truth.

And, the cost of operating the CIA to learn the truth, over 100 billion dollars per year. The cost of just asking the average citizens using Google Super Vote? Zero.

In this book, we are going to be asking the reader to think about this amazing fact of life: How the majority of people can be right over 90% of the time. Take an individual and try to get the correct response to a situation, the correct solution to a problem, and your odds are not good.

Even taking a few hundred people, and putting them in a room and asking them to solve a problem, create the proper legislation to give the correct response to a situation, and Congress has proven that your odds are not very good at all, that this size group will come up with the proper solution.

It seems that human being as flawed as they are, as individuals, need to be taken as a whole when you want to find the best solution to a problem. This is the essence of Democracy. The majority of us will be included in a majority decision for the majority of times. Sometimes, we will be in the minority decision. But, most of the time, our assessments will be the same as the majority assessment most of the time.

Another way of proving this is to look at History, which has proven over and over again, that the decisions of a small group, an insider group, the so-called elite, the elected or the anointed ones, make the poorest choices that can be made on any given situation. One only has to look at the most glaring examples of what I call the 'Exceptionally Small -Braintrust' decisions that we get every day out of our world governments.

Obamacare is the most recent example of the worst possible solution to a problem forced upon the American people by a 'Exceptionally Small -Braintrust'.

The Problem: Too many Americans Uninsured.

The Exceptionally Small -BrainTrust Solution: Spend over Two Trillion Dollars paying subsidies to people who are low-income and taxing the higher income people, forcing them to support the low-income people of this country in yet another 'Entitlement' and at a time, when the country is going bankrupt due to the level of 'Entitlements' already on the books.

Also giving the Insurance Companies the greatest boon in history by forcing people to buy their products.

NOW, here's the mental exercise that you as my reader needs to suffer for a few minutes before continuing to read the material in this book.

The question for you is this: IF Obamacare, as it is written, all TEN THOUSAND PAGES of it were put on the BALLOT for you to vote on using Google Super-Vote, would you vote for it or against?

Since the Supreme Court determined that it is a Tax upon the American People, would you vote for ANY Tax Increase given the high level of Federal, State, Local taxes that you are paying currently?

This may be too easy a question for many of you.

Here's another one: Please put yourself through this mental exercise too.

IF a proposition were placed on Google Super-Vote for the America to send over ONE HUNDRED BILLION DOLLARS in foreign aid, most of it GUNS and AMMUNITION for Dictators - would you vote FOR that or would you vote AGAINST it?

Your Congress, a 'Brain-Free Braintrust' votes to do that in your name every day. OVER one hundred billion of YOUR DOLLARS is sent to foreign nations every year and most of it is in the form of GUNS and AMMUNITION purchased with this money and sent to DICTATORS all around the world just so that they can remain in power.

The King of Saudi Arabia, for example receives over Five Billion Dollars every year in our military support. We also send

Israel about the same, Five Billion Dollars in military aid, Fighter Jets, Bombs, Guns and missiles and AMMO.

At the same time, we spend more billions with our elected officials flying all around the world telling people not to go to war with each other, even while sending them the guns and ammo to do so. If we just stopped sending them weapons and ammo, the problem would be solved. They wouldn't be able to go to war with each other.

This kind of decision making process is the result of a 'Brain-Free BrainTrust' making the decisions for the larger group.

Yet, if we put these same decisions to the test of a Real Democracy, the Google Super-Vote system, as just one example, we would have solved these problems faster, cheaper and with long lasting benefits to all parties.

Is it clear to you the reader, that the vast majority of Americans would NOT vote to send their money to foreign countries, and especially not in the form of fighter jets and missiles that can be used to harm each other. Being the good and generous people we are, we might vote to send a few million dollars to any nation that suffers from a natural disaster, as we do all the time, but probably NEVER vote FOR a proposal to send foreign dictators the weapons and ammo to war on each other, and especially knowing that sometimes, they even use our weapons against us.

Nor would the vast majority of Americans vote FOR any legislation that was described in over 10 pages of text for the very simple and common-sense reason that anything over 10 pages of text is going to be so complicated that it would be doomed to failure from the start, just as Obamacare is now so doomed. There is one provision, in Obamacare, it turns out that all you have to do is check a box somewhere that you "OPT-OUT of the system due to a hardship" and you no longer have to buy health insurance. They cannot fine you or retaliate against you, yet the whole entire premise of Obamacare is that if everyone is forced to have insurance, the economies of the largest risk pool in history would allow the insurance process to pay for the ones who get sick.

But, in the two thousand pages of the law, some numbskull stuck this provision in it that makes it null and void for those who are intelligent enough to read it and find the form where they can so choose to OPT-OUT. I am one of those.

There are many other pieces of Obamacare that make no sense at all, too many of them to enumerate here, but it will always stand in history as the best example of too small a group being allowed to create a solution to a problem.

And the other way to look at our system of problem-solving is that when you give this power to a small group, they will always choose the most expensive solution. Often, it is not only the worst solution, but also the most expensive solution. So, it's WRONG, makes the PROBLEM WORSE and is the most expensive way to MAKE A PROBLEM WORSE that you could imagine. Why? Because it's not their money. Plain and simple. They think that money grows on trees, that there is never any need to balance any books, and that all they have to do is write a check and the Federal Reserve will back them up and so they do the easiest and most expensive thing. They spend our money on the worst solutions because they know deep down, that this vicious cycle will give them another opportunity to spend even more money trying to reverse the problems that they themselves just created a while back. And even then, they will opt for the most expensive solution to a solution, that was really a worse problem they created.

Google Super-Vote is just the opposite type of system. Voting on the Internet where anyone has the ability to create their own suggestion, their own proposed solution to a problem, would in my humble opinion, very quickly lead to a system that uses the 'Wisdom of the Crowd', the general common sense that we all have to some degree and that can be used by our modern technology to arrive at the most agreed upon solution that the vast majority of people can accept and support.

The best solutions will be voted UP and the dumbest suggestions will be voted DOWN by the 'Wisdom of the Crowd' by the common sense consciousness that most of us have most of the time.

This book explains in detail how we can use Google Super-Vote or similar technology on the Internet to create the Google Super State, a euphemism that I am using in this book to highlight how easy it would be to have a form of government using Google type technology to unite us all and bring the Wisdom of the Crowd to bear on any given problem that we face today.

This idea came to me in its raw form when years ago, Richard Nixon sent me a letter requiring me to go and join his war in Viet Nam. I read about this struggle in college books and the truth was that we had no beef with these people. They were trying to free themselves from the French who had made Viet Nam a French Colony and they were paying these poor and kindest people slave wages to work in the fields.

It was an abomination of American so-called Democracy for one man, first Lyndon Johnson and then Richard 'Tricky Dick' Nixon to decide almost ALL BY THEMSELVES that we the American people should spend BILLIONS in Viet Nam helping the French maintain their Colony, even though we ourselves had fought a bloody revolution against England to free ourselves from that Colonial situation.

So, at that time, I thought to myself. "There has to be a better way to make decisions in a so-called Democracy." This one just another example of the 'Exceptionally Small -Braintrust' making decisions that make the problem worse and are the most expensive, this time in terms of lives of young American heroes who went there in the fullest of good faith thinking that their government would never do them wrong and then giving their lives in this mistaken most deadliest of judgments. Over 50,000 of my brothers went to their death in Viet Nam, stepping on a land mine, or being shot in the heart or the head by a little man who was merely defending his country against the foreign invasion decided by one American with the greatest power on Earth and with the greatest desire to abuse that power. Hundreds of thousands more of my brethren came home from that ill-conceived war losing an arm or a leg or both arms or both legs and worse.

Not to mention the millions of Viet Namese civilians who were bombed and strafed by American jet planes and B-52 bombers. We even destroyed their jungles so that we could see them better so that we could bomb and strafe them with a higher kill rate. All of this because of the decision made by one psychopathic person who we were fooled into placing into that position of power. Nixon had actually lied to the American voter by telling us that he had a "Secret Plan to End the War in Viet Nam." This was the promise that he made to get himself elected as our President.

Little did we know, that Nixon's "Secret Plan to End the War was to BOMB THEM EVEN MORE. He would bomb the ENTIRE PLANET if he could get away with it. Luckily, this maniac was finally stopped by his supporting of a foolish and amateurish BURGLARY of the offices of Daniel Ellsberg, otherwise known as Watergate.

In the end, we've been forced to apologize to that country and send them billions in reparations. We spend billions more every year helping this beautiful country recover from the damages done by us decades ago and in my opinion, we can never make up for the evil we did there.

Sadly, it didn't stop with Viet Nam. Another President, George W. Bush would lie to us again about another poor defenseless country - Iraq, and we would spend TRILLIONS this time on the decision made by yet another Psychopath who made it all the way to the most powerful job in the world.

Using the INTERNET to not only pick better people for these jobs, but also BETTER SOLUTIONS is the only hope for the future of Civilization.

Google Super-Vote is just the tip of the iceberg of what we can do to make things so much better for humanity as well as all other living things.

There is no doubt in my mind that Google Super-Vote will eventually evolve into something so elegant, so useful, so beneficial, so amazing that someday most of the world will look at what we have achieved and call it the greatest 'Wonder of the World' in all of human history.

And all of this is doable. - The United States Constitution provides that the people of the United States reserve the right to alter their form of government whenever it is shown that their present form of government no longer serves their general health and welfare.

There has never been a better time since the First American Revolution that our government must be replaced with a new one. Our leaders in Washington D.C. constantly find issues that are of no import to the American people to distract us from the real issues of jobs, taxes, transportation, the food supply, the quality of our air and water and the economy. Instead of addressing these most important issues that concern the vast majority of Americans, they find ways to waste our blood and treasure in foreign nations that have no relationship to us. Or they will find ways to argue for months and even years about Abortion, or the Palestinians, the Canadians, the Mexicans, the Australians, the Europeans, the Ukrainians, the Russians, the Chinese, the Koreans, North and South, the Cubans, the Africans, the Hungarians, the Turks, and it goes on and on.

It's never about the health and welfare and well-being of their own people, the ones they are sworn and were elected to serve. If they are so morally outraged at these events that occur overseas, then they should resign their posts as representatives of the American People and then emigrate to these foreign nations and make whatever charitable contribution they can using their own personal funds. But, when they continually waste the blood and treasure of the American People without their express or implied permission, our government has failed and it has failed us on a permanent basis.

The time has come to amend the social contract under which they, the elected and appointed government officials operate. It's time to discuss how the American people can take the reigns of political and economic power and guide their own destiny on a daily basis. The Invention of the Internet allows us to replace the old antiquated model of elected an official and then sending them to a building very far away from the origin of their power. Today, we can eliminate the middleman and tally the votes on the issues from every American citizen from the comfort of their homes or offices. In this way, we eliminate the need to send representatives who go to Washington D.C. as paupers and return a few years later as billionaires while those who elected them become poorer and poorer with every passing day. Is this democracy? Is this even a Republic any longer? It's clear to most that we now live in a dictatorship of the very rich and our government leaders are merely puppets of the very rich.

Why do we have to have a Federal Health Care Plan forced upon us which the Supreme Court called another form of taxation? Why wasn't Obamacare ON THE BALLOT to let the people decide if they really wanted to take money from the healthy people to help support the sick people in society? Why wasn't the War in Iraq on the Ballot to let the people decide if we really wanted to spend thousands of lives and trillions of dollars on removing a leader from office in Iraq simply because our leader didn't like the man personally and who was obviously making up stories about weapons of mass destruction?

Is it time to use the INTERNET to help our country make better decisions? When President Obama announced nearly a Trillion Dollar Plan to start a Federal Health Care Plan, during the worst economic conditions in history and the worst growing federal deficits, I emailed the President at the White House and I advised him that all he had to do was get the laws changed so that a corporation could be formed as a Health Care Insurance provider with minimal funding and relaxed regulations. If the President had taken my advice, there would be by now, TENS OF THOUSANDS OF NEW HEALTH INSURANCE PROVIDERS all providing competing plans to protect someone from a health challenge and this competition in the marketplace for this type of product would very rapidly bring costs down.

I'm confident that other Americans were emailing and calling the White House with even BETTER SUGGESTIONS than mine. Not one of us were consulted and not one of our suggestions THAT WOULD COST THE TAXPAYERS NO MONEY, would NOT RAISE the DEFICIT ONE DIME, and would be VOLUNTARY so that people who had good health, the vast majority of Americans, would not be subject to the tyranny of being forced to subsidize the rest of society, a small minority who had contracted a major and very expensive disease. BUT not ONE of us were consulted and ONLY the MAJAOR HEALTH INSURANCE PROVIDERS such as Aetna and Blue Cross were consulted and of course these two corporations are major sources of MONEY for both parties, and so ONLY THEIR ADVICE was sought and ONLY their ADVICE was taken.

SO NOW, we have the fiasco of Obamacare that even a four-year old could have told you wouldn't make any real progress for America in helping to solve these exploding medical care costs that is almost bankrupting this nation. Even a four-year old could have told you that Obamacare as it was crafted for us BY THE MAJOR HEALTH CARE PROVIDERS would only hasten our race to Bankruptcy as they had woven in policies that would make them even richer and more profitable than ever before.

The question THIS BOOK asks the American People: IS IT TIME TO FIND A BETTER WAY TO MAKE THIS COUNTRY'S

MAJOR POLICIES so that they impact the benefit of the MAJORITY instead of always the tiniest of MINORITIES?

After reading this book, we are going to send you to a web site where you can start making the answers to this question appear to everyone in this country so that we can all begin to work on a plan to do exactly this.

Google Super-Vote is the first glimmer of hope that we've had since the inception of this country over two hundred years ago.

Using Google Super-Vote for something much bigger than who wins a talent competition is the key to that hope becoming a reality. With your help, we can make this a reality. At the end of this book, we show you how you can help force Google to expand their use of Super-Vote into the political arena.

We have a 100% guaranteed plan that will work to get first our country back and then to put the entire world on safer footing. It's something you must do for your soul. You have the sacred duty to help make your planet a better place than how you found it. We're here to help you fulfill that duty.

ARTICLE IX of the US Constitution states:

The enumeration in the Constitution, of certain rights, shall not be construed to deny or disparage others retained by the people.

In this book, you will have a plan wherein the people can start using these other rights that we retain. Google Super Vote can be INSTRUMENTAL to educate the masses and be the starting point on a new path through future history.

Google's amazing new technology plus a few others I have in mind can and must save this country from the path to ruin that we're on. Google Super Vote would be the engine that releases at last - 'The Wisdom Of The Crowd.'

I have given this book the subtitle of 'Google Images of a New World' because I believe that when we all have the image of a real democracy in our heads, how it can save our country from the evils that have befallen it over the last fifty years of mediocre leadership at best and a Do-Nothing Congress, a rubber stamp for the Imperial Presidents, how we can use this modern technology to rule ourselves, control our insatiable appetite for greed and power, then and only then will we have reached our highest and best Evolution as a species.

I invite all of my readers to hold the concepts contained in this book closely to your hearts and minds. The images will appear in your mind of how you can join in the peaceful attainment of what I am certain God had in mind for this great nation when he gave the founding fathers their inspiration to create it in the first place.

CHAPTER ONE: Google Super-Vote

Well, now you can, that is if we can convince Google to use their wonderful technology for the Presidential Race of 2016. That will depend of course on how many people read this book and help us pressure Google into doing the right thing.

Now, how would it work to elect our Next President? Well, imagine a web site like Facebook, but instead of allowing anyone to post their face and personal profile here, we only allow people who want to run for President of the United States. Later, we can include Congressional seats as well, but in this first Online Election, we only wish to choose our President with these tools, just so we don't confuse people any more than we are already going to do with all of these crazy new-fangled ideas.

So, any of the voters can come in and create a Voter Profile, that is, they are not a candidate for office, but they want to help someone get elected to office this way or at least they're willing to check out the site and see how it compares to the silly sound bites and stuff like that that they're always going to see on TV during a campaign.

So, as the candidates post information on their web pages, their videos, their Bio's, resume's qualifications, statements of political purpose, things like that, any new kind of ideas that they want to bring to the table, the rest of the members give them votes either up or down using the Google Super-Vote widget and over time, the web site promotes those who have the most votes to the top of the ladder. It's like a tennis match where people are paired off and the winner gets to the next round until we finally have a FINALS MATCH-UP.

Pretty simple stuff. More will be worked out by other participants and web site designers, but this is the basic animal. Now, the point it, out of the thousands and thousands of ordinary citizens who think they can do a better job than the present office holder, we eventually come up with someone who probably can accomplish more because he or she is NOT tied to either the Democratic or Republican Parties.

And, there will be tens of thousands of candidates to choose from because the job pays very well and the person holding this office gets all of the perks and the power of course is pretty stuff. But, if you're over 35 years of age and you have some confidence you can do a better job of guiding this country better than the other string of losers, then, "Bob's your Uncle", let's get you a badge.

And, the sad fact is that just about anyone we pick this way is probably going to do a far better job than the last string of Presidents because when you look at how much they've accomplished during these last fifty years, it's really LESS THAN ZERO. They've in fact, taken this country backwards into the Third World classification, when we used to be the single greatest nation by far and there were no close seconds. But today, China is now the Number One economy and many other nations are rapidly catching up and the USA will soon be down in the bottom of the cellar in terms of a healthy economy. In fact, we may already be there and it's all over but the fat lady singing our woes.

Any 12 year old could do a better job as long as he or she stays honest.

Let's continue now with a Full Demonstration of How Google Super-Vote works or could work in more detail. By the end of this book, I hope to prove the statement above that any 12 year old could do a better job because under a Super-Vote Real Democracy in Action, the average person has all the power and the President really has very little power to screw things up.

You can go to one of my websites and watch a short VIDEO here. America2inc.com

What you will see in this video OR if you have ever watched American Idol and voted recently for one of their contestants, is a very nice and clean and also SECURE way created by Google to allow anyone with an Internet connection to vote in a fun and interesting way from the comforts of their home for the candidate of their choice.

Now, of course, in an actual Federal Election, the participants of Google Super-Vote would have to first prove that they were a registered voter, but there could also be a Google Page that got someone to the State Voter Registration page where they could register again from the comfort of their home and without having to visit a dusty old office in a dingy office building somewhere paying for gasoline and parking to do so.

With today's Internet technology we could register TEN TIMES as many citizens and in one tenth the time, and be 1,000 percent more assured of the identity of the voters, thus reducing voter fraud. If you are already a registered voter, it would be easy for you to verify the information that your state or local government has on you and this could all be done online. And, if you are a new citizen, it would be very easy for you to verify your identity online by simply providing copies of tax returns to the state that could come from a registered IP address where you are already verified by your ISP as the owner of that IP address.

One way or another, the potential for voter fraud is far less on today's Internet than it is under the current system where you go to a local high school and punch tabs out of a punch card system and then you hand in your ballot to someone you've never seen before in your life, someone who volunteered to help the process and for all you know that volunteer could be KGB or CIA, or even from another planet. You never ask them for their identification and yet you are handing them your ballot and they put it in a box. You have no idea where that box ends up. You never have the chance to follow that box of ballots. You have no idea if your vote is ever actually counted. This is probably how George W. Bush was elected twice. They stuffed the ballot boxes and never counted anyone who voted for the other guy. There's no way of knowing. And, you have to admit that after crashing the American economy that voters would give him a second chance, but according to our voting system, that's exactly the IRRATIONAL behavior they expect us to accept.

With all the voting tallies being online, there would be thousands of ways to check to add up all the numbers of votes from different regions

To make Google Super-Vote something more than just choosing the best candidates on American Idol, we will have to amend the

Constitution to make this type of system the law of the land. By adding this new basic freedom and power to the people, we would in essence be taking the major power of the Congress away from them and placing it in the hands of the average American citizen. Does this frighten you?

I hope not, because it should be blatantly obvious that the average American living today could make far better decisions for America than the ones coming out of Congress. If you can think of one example over the last fifty years where Congress made a decision that you can agree with, please let me know. I know of none, myself.

I don't condone foreign aid. I think that's not our responsibility. We have a tough enough time funding our own projects. This is why we're nearly 20 trillion dollars in debt. So, is foreign aid even a reasonable form of law to force upon the American people at this time? Of course not. If you think it is, you're just not thinking. Every dollar that goes out to foreign countries is a dollar that is not going to be spent here preventing the violence in our schools, helping people get to work over this nation's roads or lack of roads. None of this money will got to prevent people losing their homes. None of it will go to helping Americans escape hunger or diseases. Not one dollar of these hundreds of billions of dollars will go to help us find jobs, or to create jobs, or to build hospitals, or to help the farmers survive today's severe weather.

Not a dime of it will go toward solving these horrible pollution problems that the world faces that is destroying our ability to survive. No, none of these things will be addressed by their decisions this year or any year. Instead, these billions will find their ways into the private Swiss Bank Accounts of the dictators. Every day, the news is full of yet another discovery of another five or ten billion of our foreign aid dollars going to yet another dictator who was buying palaces all over the world, private jets, Rolex watches, Armani suits, prostitutes, while his people continued to starve to death.

Would you personally take out your wallet and give these creatures any of your money? Of course not, and yet this is what our Congress does for you in your name because they know that you have no voice, no way to prevent them to stop them from doing insane things like this every day.

They pay the oil companies. They actually pay the oil companies TRILLIONS in tax subsides over the years and here is certainly one industry that doesn't need any of our tax dollars. They already dip into our pockets every day when we fill our cars gas tanks. Yet, your Congress wants to give them even more of your money and continues to do so every day. The insanity will never stop until we provide ourselves with a way to control them, to leash them in.

Google Super-Vote is a start in that direction.

Clearly the time has come for a major change, but not just a few cosmetic changes in the way that our government looks and certainly not in changing a few of the players. It is time to call for a new version of America that is based on pure democracy, using the Internet to vote up or down the major solutions to all of our most pressing problems.

Should we raise taxes on the corporations? Should we stop all foreign aid and intervention? Should we eliminate welfare? Should we stop spending over half of our resources on war and the preparation for war? Should we make the casual use of Marijuana legal? Should we stop and even reverse the outsourcing of American jobs by American corporations? Should we eliminate the Peronal Income Tax? Should we replace the Income Tax with a National Sales Tax? Should we limit the salaries and pensions of Federal Employees to something resembling what people earn in the private sector? Should we stop the banks from gambling with depositors money? Should we make the Federal Reserve accountable for all their actions? Should we break up the monopoly of the medical practitioners and the health Insurance Industry?

Should we build more roads and bridges, instead of building infrastructure in Iraq and Afghanistan? Should we build an army of the Peace Corps instead of an army of mass destruction?

These and many other questions of the day could be solved on the Internet in FIVE DAYS, instead of the average of FIVE DECADES that our present form of government requires and when they do finally come to a conclusion, it's so full of loopholes and special interest subsidies, they create more problems than they solve in Congress today. Why not let the people decide themselves?

BREAKING NEWS: The average American voter is at least as

intelligent as the average government worker. AND - it's OUR MONEY, not theirs that we would be talking about.

The truth is that we use this form of DIRECT BALLOT INITIATIVE IN 22 STATES. Why in the name of God don't we use this on the Federal Level? It can only be because they don't want us to do that. It would cut down their power and their ability to make unauthorized sums of money. That's why. Our Government is the biggest RIP-OFF in history and it's time We The People put a stop to it.

This kind of total systemic change can only be done in a Constitutional Convention, where the majority of Americans are represented AND CAN TAKE DIRECT ACTION and SEND US THEIR INPUT over the INTERNET. Therefore, we are calling for an Internet Constitutional Convention.

If millions of Americans agree that this is an idea whose time has come, rally around this event. Share it with everyone you know. If you care about your country in any way, isn't it time you did something for your country? Isn't it time we talked about leaving a new and improved version of America to our progeny? Isn't it time we followed the lead of the founding fathers and radically changed our relationship of the governed to the governing powers?

If you agree with the statements above, there is only one thing you can do to help. That is to support this cause by purchasing tickets. The vast majority of attendees will attend by Internet Conferencing. The most qualified of our thinking people will be invited to attend in person to debate these issues.

It is clear to this author that the American system is in such a decline that its imminent demise is upon us. We are a bankrupt nation in both money and ideas. The proof of that is all around us in the form of the insane things that they are doing now in our name all over the world. The proof of our demise is that we can no longer afford to build out our own country while other countries are whizzing past us in terms of technological achievement. China, Europe and Japan, for example have trains that go over 300 Miles per hour with zero fatalities while in this country we have trains that cannot make it over 50 miles per hour and we kill over 1,000 people per year in train crashes.

Our food, air and water is being poisoned at an alarming rate even while the supply and amount of food air and water is being threatened. Our citizens are dying from cancer and other diseases from all of the pollution and we are helpless to stop or even curtail it because of the reckless spending of trillions of dollars in foreign lands. What has all of that lack of planning and leadership gotten us?

In the next version of the United States of America, these problems with their best solutions will be put to the people in the form of National Ballot Measures, and after a careful debate and research, the Voters will decide if and when to have our next foreign adventure and even how much to spend on them. In the next version of the United States of America, we will place on the ballot several of the top solutions to solve our health care problems and the people will choose the best one, the one most favorable to them, the majority. In the next version of America, we will place on the ballot whether or not WE CHOOSE to support our schools, or reduce our taxes, or even if we wish to increase our taxes in order to fund a popular project like cleaning up our nation's air or water.

In one gleaming moment that would shine brightly all around the world, We The People could decide to drive electric vehicles, replacing our gasoline powered cars. In one proud moment that would change the world, We The People could decide to end hunger in America. We could decide to end homelessness in America. We could decide to end poverty and drug use in America. Then, when we've constructed the most prosperous and healthy environment for all living things here in this country, we might even learn how to extend that prosperity and healthy living all over our God-given planet Earth.

Now is the time for all good men to come to the aid of their country. Spread the News. Let the New American Revolution BEGIN!

My views are of course my views. There are millions of other Americans who may have ideas even better than some of the ones you will read about here. The major point I'm making here is that in a Real Democracy, only the BEST IDEAS would make it to the top of the pile and then we ALL DECIDE who's ideas are to become the law of the land. Yes, we will make mistakes at times and shoot ourselves in the foot. But one must ask, could ordinary citizens shoot themselves in the foot as often as our elected village idiots in Washington D.C. shoot us all in the foot?

AND, even if we do shoot ourselves in the foot on occasion, it would be very easy to overturn our own flawed decisions and reverse ourselves whenever it became obvious that We The People had made such a mistake.

You can be one of the founding fathers or mothers of America 2.0, Inc. We can't just sit around and wait for the two Parties to complete the destruction of the greatest country that ever existed. President Clinton began the destruction of the global economy by eliminating the law known as Glass-Steagall, set in place during the Great Depression and it saved the country. But, Clinton's Wall Street Advisors whispering in his ear and tempting him with visions of hundreds of millions of dollars in the Clinton Bank Account, were able to use this appeal to the Clinton Greed to abolish the one law that had been working extremely well since the Great Depression to prevent another one.

After Clinton abandoned us to the greed of Wall Street in the last few weeks of his Administration, it was left to George W. AMBUSH to complete the task of sending us all down the road to Financial Armageddon which we are all enjoying today. The point is, how does so much power, the power to destroy the entire Global Banking System fall onto the shoulders of such few men, and men who have vested interests in letting us all 'Eat Cake? If you think you know the answer, you could be right, but in my opinion, they are able to foster so much power in such a few empty immoral people, only because we allow it to happen. We are sheep and we don't know what to do about any of these things, so we keep our noses to the grindstone and let them screw us over again and again.

Well, it may be too late to stop this destruction, however, somehow I believe that something better will rise up out of the ashes and I call that America 2.0 Inc. As I complete the writing of this book, FaceBook has gone public with an IPO, or initial public offering of some 425 Million Shares priced at $38 Per Share which gave Facebook a total value of over 100 Billion US Dollars. A few college pranksters who happened to know something about programming a computer, a few years back, decided that it would be fun to have a place on the Internet where anyone could post pictures of their friends and tell all their friends what they were doing every FREAKING minute of their humdrum lives.

Somehow, this crazy bit of programming resulted in making these dozen or so merry college kids multi-billionaires in just a few years. My question is, if a small group of college kids can incorporate and strike it rich on the Stock Market, shy can't a country of 350 million people, some smarter, some not as smart as Mark Zuckerberg and his band of merry college pranksters?

Well, of course the answer is: There is no reason why we can't incorporate the entire country of citizens nor is there any really sound logic against it, as far as I can tell. My book, completely original argues that the US Constitution must be amended one more time to Incorporate the Country so that our elected officials are held accountable. Normal business rules and ethics would be applied. They would have a fiduciary responsibility to us, the American People to do the right things that end up making a profit each year, instead of throwing our hard earned money down a rat hole as they do now. Your first impression is that this sounds crazy, but incorporation of the United States Government is the only way out of our 100 Trillion dollar national debt. (Not 16 Trillion as they would have us believe.) No one could ever pay this debt. But, rather than go bankrupt and ruin the "Full faith and credit" and the integrity of the greatest country ever created, we CAN simply incorporate the entire Government. This would convert all of this ridiculous debt that can never be paid off into EQUITY. And our debtors, mainly China and Japan would simply have to WAIT to get their money back from the growth of our economy.

That's just the beginning. More importantly who are the shareholders of this the greatest economy in history? Certainly not those who own stock in GM and FORD. It's you and me, babe - EVERY CITIZEN who toils to make a living and helps create the Gross Domestic Product. But, instead of being paid back in dividends and stock options, our government tosses us a few meager trinkets because we're stupid and we work to make the 1% rich, while we live on dreams. Well, we don't have to take that any more. Since we are the greatest, strongest, most productive, cleverest, most innovative, most inventive people in history, is there any doubt in your mind that the value of our Stock in America 2.0 Inc. would do nothing but go UP and UP and UP in value?

There's no doubt in this author's mind and with this book, we can begin to get our country back, both in terms of our rights and our freedoms but also in terms of MONEY. We are the shareholders of America today, they used your money and mine to bail out the banks and the Auto Companies and Insurance companies. They are using your money and mine to force everyone onto a national healthcare plan. They have spent TRILLIONS of YOUR MONEY building the economies of foreign nations. What did we get back for our investment? NOT ONE RED PENNY.

Isn't it time we get something for all our hard work? And isn't it time we forced the government to stop all their losing ideas and get to work on winners? Isn't it time THEY worked for US? Help Kick Start the 2nd American Revolution. GIVE a COPY of this book to everyone you KNOW. It pays to remember the dedication of our founding fathers who risked their lives for your freedom and liberty. The Original Declaration of Independence - 1776 "We hold these truths to be self-evident, that all men are created equal, that they are endowed by their Creator with certain unalienable Rights, that among these are Life, Liberty and the pursuit of Happiness." Every school child has this Preamble to the US Constitution drilled into their heads.

What we are not told is that these words are now obsolete and have been replaced by the operating policies of the American Government of the United States ever since the turn of the last century when corporations began to buy our politicians for the paltry sum of just a few hundred dollars each. The secret mission of almost all politicians in this country today is to simply enrich themselves and their family and friends as much as they can possibly get away with before being kicked out of office.

The proof of this is the plethora of office building all up and down the major streets of Washington D.C. such as 'K' street where tens of thousands of paid lobbyists work from sunup to sundown locating Congressmen and women and pay them sums of money or jobs promised after they leave office in return for legislation, earmarks, amendments to bills that will make their client companies a fortune. The general welfare of the public is no longer a top priority in Congress and this is why this country is rapidly headed off a cliff. We can all sense the drift towards oblivion, but we are all frustrated at what we can do about it, since everyone we elect to high office, Democrat, Republican, or Independent is destined to fall into the same selfish trap of representing only themselves.

There is ONE SOLUTION as I see it, short of a violent Revolution and that is to Incorporate the United States of America, turn a non-profit losing proposition with the worst management in history into a for-profit Corporation with all the accounting requirements and full disclosure to shareholders US (More on Stocks and the Shareholders later) that is expected today and use all of the business acumen that we've learned over the centuries to make all our lives prosperous. I call it - America 2.0 Inc.

I believe that the only way out of this current economic chaos brought upon us by our two political parties is for the United States to convert to a Publicly Owned Stock Corporation. Think about it. We're basically formed as a Non-Profit which means that all politicians have the misdirected, horribly flawed way of thinking that the Government should LOSE MONEY every year. So, they do their best for us to LOSE OUR MONEY every year and they have made it an art form as a measure of their "Success in office" Both parties are guilty of this. They just lose money for different ideologies and constituencies.

If the United States of America were formed as a For-Profit Corporation instead:

1. We could convert all of our debt to equity in one simple transaction. The Chinese and other nations holding our Treasury Bonds would now be stockholders. Their own economic interests and ours would now be connected to each other.

2. We could reward citizens for public service and private service with stock in America 2.0 - in lieu of entitlements. We receive say 100 shares for being born here. Another 100 shares for keeping a job more than a year. Another 100 shares for five years consecutive job tenure. Another 100 shares for inventing something useful. Etc.

3. We would force a balanced budget and a healthy economy because officers of the corporation would be bonused every year they made a profit, and fired every year they didn't, (other than years of national emergencies)

4. We would have full disclosure and transparency in Government because everyone is a STOCKHOLDER, not just a voter and they vote their shares. The more shares earned, the more influence on policy.

5. Personal Military Adventures like Viet Nam and Iraq, would be a thing of the past because there is no profit in that. Many other ridiculous adventures, such as foreign aid, farm subsidies to NOT to grow food etc. would fade too unless there was profit in it.

6. The American people would be served, instead of ripped off by a government which is forced to profit on all it's ventures instead of trying their hardest to lose our money with no accountability, then ask us for more.

7. Financially Sound business principles, as the government's fiduciary responsibility of making us all WEALTHY would have to be followed by the government, otherwise they are fired by the stockholders in regular stockholder meetings. (Like our current Elections. But instead of rubber stamping the two parties, we would actually vote up or down on officers and policies.)

8. The Government would report to the shareholders every year with a complete and audited Balance Sheet and Profit and Loss statement. Profits are distributed to the shareholders every year. Thus we would eliminate the Income Tax and instead pay the citizens DIVIDEND CHECKS each year. The economy would now based on a cooperative effort for the country to PROFIT every year so that we maximize our yearly dividends from the IRS.

This business model would incentivize everyone to work hard instead of the current system that gives incentives to goof off. Corporate subsidies, Unemployment Insurance, Social Security, all entitlements are rendered obsolete and replaced by shares in America 2.0.

This kind of radical change can only come about as the result of a Constitutional Convention where we would bring a series of amendments to a vote of all the states. This should be the long-term goal of this organization, because a completely patriotic and independent movement can have no other long term goal other than radical changes. I see in this move as the best first step in getting our country back that is out there today.

If we simply continue down the path we're on, there is no light at the end of the tunnel. We will always be governed in a chaotic hodge-podge way such as exists today and nothing would improve. Just more bureaucracy is created. That's how they solve a problem.

When the World Trade Center were blown apart by the 19 guys who took over 4 jetliners, the response of the government should have been to find the 19 perpetrators and bring them to justice, either dead or alive, it wouldn't matter much to most of us. Then, you strengthen all the doors to the cockpits of all jetliners so that no unauthorized persons can gain access to the cockpits again. Thirdly, you watch who you're allowing into this country with a more careful scrutiny of passports. All of the 19 9/11 hijackers were on NO-FLY LISTS because of their known association with terror organizations, but none of the 100,000 people in the State Dept. whose job it is to check passports and measure them against their own no-fly lists did their jobs. NOT A SINGLE ONE OF THEM.

Several FBI agents had even learned of their plans to hijack planes because they had been reported by Flight Training schools that these 19 guys were interested in learning only how to fly a jetliner, not at all interested at how to land one. These FBI agents who warned their headquarters about this knowledge were ignored and even FIRED for doing their jobs.

So, instead of reforming the agencies that let us down in 9/11 at a cost of hundreds of billions of dollars over the years, they decide to add a new bunch of bureaucrats and call it "Homeland Security" and these guys are now busy strip searching American citizens at all airports instead of doing their original jobs. They've made life intolerable to frequent flyers, which does nothing to help our economy.

I could go on and on about government bureaucracy. The dept. of Energy has not once found us any new sources of energy and instead just invests in useless ideas and loses our money.

The Dept. of Education has not helped improve the education in this country and instead has supervised the 'Dumbing Down of America". More kids drop out of high school today than at any other time in our history. Yet we spend hundreds of billions of dollars on a Dept of Education. Why? Because this is how a Non-Profit Organization works. You get money and you spend it with no regard to the people who donated the money. In fact, in our government system of Lose-All-The-Money-You-Can-As-Quickly-As-You-Can or you're fired, the agencies get allocated more and more money and do less and less with it. If they don't spend it all, they lose it, so they work very hard at making more and more inventive ways to spend it like the recent $800,000 junket to Las Vegas where they had strippers and magicians entertain them. The head of the agency in question, also spent 8 trips of his own getting the big trip organized by having lavish parties in Las Vegas for himself, his family, his friends at a cost of another $800,000. What do we get for all this money? The answer is simple. NOTHING.

Candidate for President Barack Obama promised us "Real Change that we can believe in." Sadly, he has yet to deliver on that promise, unless his definition of change is worsening problems, more unemployment, more senseless wars, more financial and economic crises, because that's all he has delivered since becoming President. I can say these things with a great deal of credibility because I worked hard to help elect Barack Obama because I took him at his word, allowed myself to get fooled again by the fancy speeches. I donated my time and my money to his campaign, thinking that the Bush policies would be immediately reversed once Obama took office. This was my interpretation of his promise for real changes. Instead, I was saddened to find that Barack Obama meant that change might come some day. He just told us in a recent speech that this was what he meant, and we shouldn't have taken him so seriously. He was only kidding. He thought we knew that he was kidding and that maybe in his second term there could be real change.

There is no change under this or any other American President because the system is so totally corrupt there is no way to get any justice for the American middle class. And, that's why i can say that America version 1.0 is dead. I know this is shocking news to most of you. But, when you really think about it, taking off the rose colored glasses, this is the reality we are in. BUT, when the King dies in the old feudal system, there is a new successor King or Queen and we have that in America 2.0, thank God. Long live the King. Long Live America 2.0, Inc.

Origin of the CONCEPT:

I first started thinking about REAL Democracy in America during the Viet Nam War. I had just graduated college. I was a healthy young man at the age of 22 and the Viet Nam War was raging. On the news every night were images of American soldiers, young kids like me really, being ordered to go into a Viet Nam village and assassinate all the people in that village, men, women and children or they were being blown to bits by mortars coming out of nowhere or had legs and arms blown off by mines.

If you were fighting on the ground, you were ordered to do these things with your own rifle and grenades and flame throwers. You were told these were "The Enemy" and it was your patriotic duty to eradicate these people. They were either Communists or supporting the communists by feeding them and giving them shelter in their villages. Nothing was further from the truth, but this is the story that our boys were brainwashed with in Boot Camps and in the country.

I thought to myself, "Is this really what America stands for?" And, "How many Americans would support the mass murder of these poor unfortunate people?" I had no scientific data on this. They weren't even conducting polls on the subject. The media didn't want to seem "Unpatriotic", so very little was said out in the open at first. The media just went along with the White House Lyndon Johnson and then worse than him, Richard Nixon, that these people were evil and we had to do something about it.

When, I did my research on the subject, however, I came up with a completely different conclusion. These people had been subject to the French as part of their Colonial Empire for over 200 years. They had been abused, enslaved, their women raped by their French masters. They were paid, if they were paid at all, about 25 cents per day to do the dirty work in the mines and on the plantations that French people did not want to do. Sound familiar? They were not armed or militant in any way, so the French knew that they could keep them down without any real worries or even any adverse publicity.

Then, the Viet Namese started to get some weapons from the Russians and Chinese to the North and they decided to stand up for themselves. So, they fought the French in their own War of Independence and their model was the American Revolution of 1776. They looked to us for aid and support. They even wrote an early Constitution that was a carbon copy of the American Constitution they had their heroes just like George Washington and Thomas Jefferson and James Madison and even Ben Franklin who they worshipped.

They hoped and prayed that someday America would come to their aid. But, someone in the Pentagon, when they got the request for Support from the Viet Namese people revolting against their French enslavers, got the idea that this would be a good place to test our new generation of military weapons, the new rifles, bombs, tanks, airplanes, explosives etc. So, we took a stand with the French, the Oppressors instead of the Oppressed, and thereby became the oppressors, the enslavers, the invaders, the mass murderers. They were Asian, had slanty eyes, didn't wear much clothes, didn't go to school, lived mainly in grass huts, so they would be no match for our firepower and we could show the world how powerful and innovative the American military was.

We would intimidate the Russians and the Chinese so they would know just how tough and smart we were. This was the Pentagon Policy and it was fed to the American people through the media and even through the mouths of Lyndon Johnson first, and then Richard M. Nixon so that the American people would not hear the truth. Nixon expanded the war and murdered ten times the people that Johnson had murdered. Nixon even ordered the expansion of the war into Cambodia after telling the American people during his 2nd term campaign that he had a 'Secret End to the War' and that it would end when he got Re-Elected. This deceit worked.

The real candidate who would have ended the war, George McGovern was out maneuvered by Nixon who stole the votes of the American Electorate claiming that he would end the war "With Honor", while McGovern would have just recalled all the troops and somehow this would dishonor our country. The American people bought this subterfuge and so Nixon won a 2nd Term and increased the murder and destruction of the area using B-52 Bombers, jet fighters that would strafe the women and children, and drop Napalm, a terror weapon that laid the entire village, jungle, rice patties, everything for miles around them in violent flames that would actually attach to the skin of any poor animal that was in the vicinity, burning them to death or disfiguration at the least.

The jungle burned to the ground for years from our heinous and immoral incendiary bombs. More bomb tonnage was dropped on that poor unfortunate country than all of the tons of bombs in World War II. Millions of innocent men, women and children were murdered, burned beyond recognition, vaporized, slaughtered like pigs in the name of American despotism. Millions of square miles of rain forest, thousands of villages were poisoned and depleted and destroyed. They poured thousands of tons of defoliant on the trees and brush so that the bombers could see their targets better.

This defoliant, Agent Orange, is still polluting the rivers and streams of this beautiful country and even found in the fish all over the planet. They caused all of this ecological damage and mass murder of millions of poor defenseless people under the guise that they were a threat somehow to the interests of the United States. I could see no threat to my country, and neither did millions of other Americans. We protested. We sent letters. We saturated Congress with phone calls and complaints. We wrote letters to the editors. We wrote books, made documentaries. Some of us even became violently opposed to this war in total frustration, but We The People who were financing this mass murder were never able to change anything, until the Viet Namese finally became strong enough to kick our troops out of their country.

This defeat is the biggest military upset in the history of the world, surpassing even the famous battle at Thermopolye were 300 Spartans held back the Persian army of one hundred thousand troops for about ten days, until they were finally overwhelmed. Remember, not a single American citizen voted for this war. Only a few ignorant and easily brainwashed Americans were in support of this war. Few of us had any idea why our troops were sent there and why they were forced to fight and die in the pursuit of killing people who were in revolt against the dictatorship first of France, who held them as a colony and then an American Puppet regime. (America was a colony that revolted against England. But our leaders don't study history or don't care to learn its lessons, I guess.)

The Viet Name people who started out with nothing but stones and spears, defeated the most powerful nation on Earth, a nation that could have obliterated them with one order of the Commander-In-Chief. Thank God, that order never came. But, we were damned close. It has recently come to light of day, that Richard Nixon was considering ending the war "Honorably" by ordering the use of the Atomic Bomb on these poor people. As luck would have it, he became embroiled in the Watergate scandal where he was caught authorizing a petty burglary of Daniel Ellsberg's office.

Imagine, the President of the United States complicit in a petty burglary. These are the kinds of people we were and still are controlled by. At least the Mafia is up front about their crimes. The American government manages to hide them from us because they are in bed with the major media outlets. The point of all this background is that, besides protesting and calling our Congress and writing letters, I also tried to convince everyone that these kinds of issues should get on the ballot. My argument was and still is, that a nation with all of this power and responsibility cannot ever allow a single person, a Lyndon Johnson or a Richard Nixon lead us into this kind of moral and economic morass.

Few listened and today We The People have just as little control over our government as we had back then, when we were led down the path of all this horror and waste of human blood and treasure in Viet Nam. George W. Bush was the proof of that. Taking his queue from the fact that Nixon and Johnson were never punished for their lies and deceit and murder, believed he could get away with this type of behavior too by lying again to the American People to get us into his favorite little adventure the War in Iraq.

But Bush was even better at this than Nixon. Nixon only wasted 100 Billion Dollars in Viet Nam. Of course the cost is still growing for Viet Name with the continually growing expense of Veterans Pensions and Health Care benefits. But, Bush was able to squander 200 TIMES the cost of Viet Nam. So far this war in Iraq has cost us over One Trillion dollars and by the time we rebuild Iraq and finish compensating all the Veterans returning home from Iraq and Afghanistan PLUS all the war materials suppliers, it will run up to a total of at least Two Trillion Dollars.

Never mind the costs to the Reputation of the greatest and most democratic country that ever lived. Never mind the money, but this wastefulness and other wasteful policies of the last 50 years has also cost us the greatest economic boom in history and brought us all to our knees. We are now at the level of a third world nation, the largest debtor nation in the world, and the most rapidly declining in terms of quality of life, infrastructure, prosperity.

Most other nations of the world are growing economically now while we are in a decline and this is 100% the results of decisions made by lunatics who have somehow gained the most powerful office, United States Congressman or woman and President of the United States.

Where did it all go wrong? When we let them get away with this. And we let these people get away with this insanity because we are part of a NON-PROFIT, LOSE AS MUCH MONEY AS YOU CAN TYPE ORGANIZATION. Therefore, it's almost criminal to suggest that these people are doing anything wrong. They're just being highly efficient at losing our money, our reputation, our freedoms too, by the way, but it's sort of PART OF THEIR CHARTER. You have the entire legal establishment lining up against you if you tried to suggest they do anything else. In a For-Profit type of CHARTER the opposite would be true.

So – This has to stop now of there is no more America as the founding fathers had intended it. We must take the power of controlling ourselves back from the people who have proven throughout history that they have no desire to serve us. They serve only their own whims about ethics and right and wrong.

And here's the IRONY of it all. In a real democracy, the people should have more to do and to say about the way things are done, are they not? Yet, in this country, proven by the Viet Nam War Protests and the protestations about the Iraq war, the protestations we have every day about the economic policies - THEY IGNORE IT ALL. This is no democracy, not even close. It's supposed to be a Republican or Representative Form of Democracy, but when the average and moral and bill-payers are ignored completely, it's not even that weakest form of democracy for the people who are supposed to represent us, the average guy, are now representing the arms merchants, the drug pushers, the military, the oil companies, the telephone companies, the car manufacturers and not much else.

OH, no they also seem to represent gay people in one sense that they have ended the 'Don't ask, Don't tell policy in the Armed forces. And, then on the other hand, they represent the religious right by also trying to make gay marriage illegal. So, sometimes they represent certain interests, but these are not the interests that really matter, at least not to me. My guess is that they throw these minor issues out there to prove to us that they are trying to do something for us, but these are insignificant rule changes that mean nothing to the welfare of the average American citizen or to our rights to a free and democratic society. The more un-important little things they give us the more we think they may be OK kind of guys. They're clever. You have to give 'em that.

AND, if it takes them decades to solve even these smallest of problems, such as whether or not someone in the Army or Navy Air Force or Marines should tell anyone they are gay - imagine how long it will take them to solve a real problem that effects us all, such as balancing the budget, whether or not to get our troops out of harms way and save our country and our troops lives?

Imagine how long it will take them to solve a problem like how to convert our cars and trucks to Natural Gas and take all the political power away from the oil companies, drug companies, telecom companies, etc.?

These are the real problems facing us for decades and it will be decades longer before they resolve them and only after it has cost us our nation. Gay people in the armed forces have been an issue ever since the country was formed, and THEY STILL ARGUE how they are supposed to serve. They don't have a real solution to anything. It's just more insanity.

Fix something and MOVE-ON to the NEXT PROBLEM, is what the government's motto should be, but sadly it's Don't FIX SOMETHING until it's too late. That's the motto of the day in all governments of the world, especially this one.

Someone should inform them that we now have electricity, computers and the Internet, so there are ways to put BETTER IDEAS on the INTERNET and VOTE ON THEM. The ideas will come from ordinary folks, like you and me, however and that's why they are fighting real changes like this, that are so obvious to them as well as to us. They like having the power completely in their hands and they will resist to their last breath in relinquishing any of it to us. But, things are happening now that you, dear reader are going to become aware of. Changes are taking place right now at a pace much faster than even our government can control.

Take heart America. These changes are coming and it's solely due to the freedom of the Internet, the lack of control that our government has over these ideas, that will be our salvation. Do not despair. Change is coming, whether those currently in power like it or not. At the end of this book, you will be informed about all of it and how you can help make it happen. I trust in the wisdom of ordinary people to make the changes that are necessary when they are finally pushed to the wall. We have our backs at that wall today. Time to push back.

When still a candidate for President of the Untied States, Barack Obama put on the masthead of his web site, "I'm not asking that you place your faith in me to make the big changes in Washington. I'm asking that you place your faith in yourselves to make these changes." When I read these words, my mind exploded with inspiration for many new ideas for our government and I sent the Obama Administration this idea as well as dozens of others just as helpful. After four years of the Obama Administration I have yet to hear back. Surely there needs to be a better way for Citizens of a Democracy to control their politicians and hold them accountable for their misdeeds, incompetence, lack of vision, narrow-mindedness, and their almost universal outright greed for personal power.

AND, the promised changes have yet to arrive. In a recent statement, after being told by Google, Microsoft, Yahoo, AOL and ten other of the biggest Internet firms, that SPYING on Americans by the NSA would destroy the Internet, President Obama said he would study the matter. After three months of "Study", he announced recently that instead of the Federal Spy Agency keeping the data that they got by spying on us themselves, they would store it with the major Phone Companies. He just shifted the spying that was being collected from one hard drive to another. If that's the kind of change he was talking about, he should have used different wording. Like "Change that you can't really trust, but we'll do something. Take it or leave it." That's apparently the kind of change he was talking about.

Because if it weren't for Whistle Blower Edward Snowden, we would never have learned that the government is wasting over one hundred billion dollars every year, spying on Americans under the guise of "Protecting us".

There's a better way to make our national decisions and policies and I'm here to suggest that Google Super-Vote is an opening that we MUST go through.

At the end of this book, we have a one hundred percent guaranteed system that will force Google and the other Internet Biggies to give this country the Real Democracy that we deserve, the real democracy that our forefathers fought and died for. Please take this journey with me all the way to the end so that you can help us achieve this great thing. It's your duty as a living human being, having been given the gift of life on this planet to help leave it a better place than how you found it. You're not just here to take up space and use the precious resources, enjoying your life without giving back.

CHAPTER TWO: So You Want To Run For President

So far, I think it's obvious to most of my readers what the Google Super-Vote engine could do for America and most Americans. But, in this chapter, I'd like to flesh out exactly how it would feel to be an American in what I call - The Super States of America. Remember, everything I'll be proposing is based on the technology of the Internet being applied in the most Free and Democratic ways.

So - What would the Super States of America be like to live in?

First, you would no longer hear so many people complaining on the streets and in your neighborhood or on TV, because there would be nothing to complain about except perhaps how the last vote we made didn't quite solve the problem we were all trying to solve, and so we all need to go back to the drawing board.

The people who love to complain would be extremely bored. The TV Pundits like Bill O'Reilly, Hannity, Wolf Blitzer, Anderson Cooper and especially Rush Limbaugh would also be out of business. These types of people who really don't care about us and are only in the biz to make huge obscene amounts of money and so finally, they would have to get real jobs, doing something far more productive for society. One example TV show we may see these people produce would be a SURVIVOR type of show, where people are put on an island and the game is that they have to solve a global world problem like the one we suffer right now where everyone is dumping their garbage into the ocean, and killing the lungs of the planet.

Just as one example, let's say that someone proposes that we establish a "Gobal Protection Agency', something that is funded by the major culprits in the dumping of garbage and toxins into the oceans, the power companies, who pour billions of tons of mercury and other harmful chemicals into the ocean. Why don't we make them pay to clean up their own mess? And, why don't we make them pay so much that they would be forced to change their ways? The Oil Companies are another fiend who we should be fining every single day in the billions of dollars to force them to stop dumping oil and gasoline and other toxic chemicals into the oceans. If it costs them more to clean up their messes than it would for them to safer pipelines and safer ships, than it does for them to pay the fines, eventually they will become responsible citizens of the Earth.

What if there were a proposal like that staring you in the face someday on the Federal Election Ballot, the same one that allows you right now to vote for either Tweedle-Dee or Tweedle-Dummer? How would you vote? Instead today, that kind of legislation can never even make it to the floor of our Congress because there is always one man, one woman, one person who gets to chair the committee that's in charge of this type of law. And, of course, who do the oil companies bribe first and foremost and most often? The committee chair persons because if this kind of legislation never makes it to the floor of Congress for a vote, they don't have to bribe anyone else.

What if someone put a proposal on the Internet to abolish the Federal Income Tax Code, every word of it and replace it with the following Tax Code: "As of this date forward, the United States Personal Income tax code, is replaced with the Federal Flat Tax. Every person earning income of any kind, shall pay a flat tax of 10% which employers shall be deduct from their salaries and deposit with the United States Treasury to fund the Federal Government. Any income that is derived from any source other than a wage or salary, shall be paid by the earner on a quarterly basis and shall be deposited to the United States Treasury by the taxpayer."

Now do you see the usefulness of a Real Direct Democracy. If you tried to get this kind of a simple reform of our current income tax system, it would bankrupt you as you would have to bribe Senator after Senator to get them just to consider your proposal. After many millions of your bribery dollars, they still would not do this because there would be many more millions coming to them from the Tax Attorney's Associations and Tax Accountant's Associations to counter-act every dollar you had to spend to get their attention. The big money will always prevail in our current form of non-democracy, or what I call the 'Dollar Dictatorship'.

Yet, I guarantee that if this proposal were on the Google Super Vote Ballot, ninety percent of Americans would vote for it. It would pass overwhelmingly by a huge margin because most people are fed up with having to fill out these horrific forms every April fifteenth.

So, in this example, the person who comes up with the best solution moves on. Let's say it's this one. So, the mass consciousness would be slowly raising itself from the horribly oppressive dumbing and numbing shows on TV like the Kardashian dramas to more enlightening and spiritually brilliant shows like that one. There would be many others. People would start reading good books again, instead of the trash produced by celebrities to make more money and get more famous. Schools would flourish once again and very few would drop out because having an education would be relevant again. If you didn't have a highly developed brain, you would not be able to get everything out of the Internet that you needed. With an education, practically everyone will be allowed to participate and none will be barred entry.

Homelessness, Poverty, The Welfare State, all would be drastically reduced, and eventually eliminated. How can I say that? Because these are all simply problems that the 'Exceptionally Small BrainTrust' has caused because they simply don't have enough brain power to solve tough problems like this, nor do they care about anyone except themselves.

However, when, you put the energy and imagination, innovation and creativity of millions of people to work on even these tough problems, there is no doubt they will be solved. It only takes time and the right mix of ideas that finally produce the desired results. If you doubt this, then, you don't possess these qualities and that's because you are probably the victim of the current educational system, which again, will be forced to change in order to rise to the level of expectations the new Super States of America will impose upon us all.

Now, let me demonstrate in more detail how the Super-Vote Super State would operate using recent headlines to point out the usefulness of such a system.

Let's say that a President of the United States decided that it would be a good idea to start a war in Iraq because perhaps and maybe they had evidence that this was the enemy responsible for the bombing of the World Trade Center and that they also were acquiring 'Weapons of Mass Destruction'.

Immediately upon the President announcing his intentions and putting these words out to the Community for credibility testing, the Super-Vote System would go to work.

First, some young and non-mainstream journalist, a blogger perhaps, would put up a Blog on the Super-Vote Web Site challenging the President's assertions. He may even propose a plan where people send him the money to go to Iraq and validate the President's assertions. It might be something much simpler, like checking the Newspaper report that the President used, some jerkwater rag in Africa somewhere, probably a CIA run operation, who had planted this story. And perhaps a simple SKYPE INTERVIEW of this story's publisher might reveal the truth without any expenditure of money. If that didn't shed enough light on the lies that were being perpetrated by the President, then perhaps a trip to Iraq to find the elusive 'Weapons of Mass Destruction' by a qualified group of inspectors would have been in order.

Then, the Super-Vote populace would vote that proposal either UP or DOWN. With trillions of dollars at stake of our money and hundreds of thousands of lives at stake, the American people would most likely overwhelmingly PASS this journalists proposal.

And, within a few days or weeks, and before the President would have the rubber-stamp Congress pass the necessary resolutions and funding bills for such a war, we would have our results of that research.

THEN, the Super-Vote Site would have a huge Challenge-Vote for President Bush to have to withstand. Overwhelmingly, now that we the voters new the truth, his proposal to have a war in Iraq would undoubtedly be SQUASHED. Bush would be disgraced publicly and he may even be forced to resign for lying to the American people and conspiring to defraud us the way he did. OR, failing that much anger, perhaps he could have survived the rest of his first term, but he certainly would not have been re-elected with this stain on his record. Of that, I am certain.

The economy would have been spared the worst recession in history also, under this 'Super Vote - Super States of America' scenario because it was during Bush's second term that he managed to collapse the world economy by allowing Wall Street to regain the power to defraud every major investor in the world using 'Derivatives'.

Thus, it can be seen using recent history and the facts of this case that The Google Super-Vote 'Super States of America' would be a much better place to live in. In this one example, we avert the costliest war in US History in terms of money wasted - over Two TRILLION dollars, and the costliest war in history in terms of the reputation and good faith and credit of the United States. If The United States of America can avert a total Bankruptcy as a direct result of the Bush Fraud on the world, it will be a miracle. So far, up to the date of publication of this book, we've been managing to avoid it. But, there are still signs that we may still be quietly sailing over the abyss.

And, if the United States of America is to go down the tubes and joins the Soviet Union, as ideas that just couldn't make it, is there any doubt that the world would be a much more dangerous place?

I want to focus the reader's mind on this one trend in recent history where ONE INDIVIDUAL could have such a negative impact on the world. Millions of people lost their homes due to the Bush frauds. Millions of people were murdered by American bombs due to the fraudulent decision of this one man. Millions of people lost their jobs due to the fraud perpetrated upon the world by ONE MAN. Millions of people are still suffering an economic or personal loss perpetrated upon them by ONE MAN. Millions of people will continue to suffer for decades to come because of this ONE MAN who had the power to do the most ill-advised actions that he must have known or should have known would be so detrimental.

Let's say that a Serial Killer had been the perpetrator of this kind of destruction. Is there no doubt that this man would eventually be brought to justice? Yet, just because this perpetrator managed to maneuver his way into the most powerful office in the world, we let his deeds go unpunished? Under the new Super States of America, this kind of series of unfortunate events would never have taken place. AND if they had, they would have been dealt with so swiftly as to render them harmless.

I can prove both of these statements. Under the Google Super-Vote system, can you imagine someone of George W. Bush's qualifications even getting into the semi-finals? Of course not. Under a Google Super-Vote System, thousands of highly qualified people could apply for the job of President of the United States. The ones with the best qualifications, business experience, college degrees, a background in the Sciences or a person of great achievements in life like Bill Gates or Warren Buffet, Elizabeth Warren, even someone like Barbara Bush, who recently said, "The world doesn't need any more Bushes' and wow was she right. What honesty! She knows what a mess her own son made of the world and is open and frank and honest enough to admit it.

So, given that the world is chock full of more qualified people than George W. Bush, if he had placed his hat in the ring of hundreds of better people, is there any doubt that he would have made it to any kind of run-off election? Of course not. He was a spoiled brat who had run two businesses into bankruptcy, the minute he arrived on the scene. He failed in college and he was an alcoholic. Those were his only accomplishments at the time. Under the Two-Party system where we get to choose between two BOZOS, the Bozo who is able to pull the wool over our eyes the best - WINS.

And, this is how this brainless idiot made it to the highest office in the world. Under a Google Super-Vote system where anyone may apply, this type of person would never stand a chance, because he would have to run on his resume, his experience, his background his accomplishments, not on the lies the Republican Party was able to publish successfully about him. And, since the other guy he ran against had no willingness to show us the truth, Bush won. And this horrific and antiquated system of complete decay and corruption allowed the subsequent events to transpire, the ruination of us all.

But, the Google Super-Vote system doesn't just help us find better people for the job. It also forces us to utilize better ideas. It utilizes the Greatest Brain Trust in history, the brains of all human beings combines on the Internet every day to produce amazing things like Facebook, Google, Twitter, LinkedIn, Youtube, Pinterest, etc. So, I can easily envision a Super States of America that is a combination of all these useful devices on the Internet mixed in with an even higher calling, the mission to make the world a sustainable place for all living things and thus by default eliminating the greed and corruption, things like the senseless and careless killing of dolphins and whales for personal and/or corporate greed, the pollution of our air and water for greed, sales of weapons all over the world for greed, all of these things would be suppressed because these are not in the interest of the average every day citizen.

The vast majority of us desire to breathe clean air, to drink pristine water, to be safe from harmful chemicals, to live free of fear, to be allowed to pursue our dreams. These are the every day goals of the average person. We don't need billions of dollars to have all these things either. It's those who are encouraged by our present system and who are unrestrained in their greed that cause all the major problems we face as a civilization today. It's GREED, plain and simple that needs to be controlled and curbed and discouraged. In the Super States of America, We the average citizen would finally have the power to control these aberrant and in most cases criminal individuals doing so much harm to society, just so that they can live in ten palatial homes all over the world and travel to them in private jets that consume thousands of gallons of jet fuel polluting the air the rest of us must breathe just so that he or she can enjoy this criminal form of life-style.

I can say this form of lifestyle is criminal because whenever the behavior of an individual harms any others, it should be considered a crime against humanity and must be curtailed. Here's an example of how we can criminalize the aberrant behavior that is destroying our planet, slowly but surely.

One or maybe a group of us gets a notion that Fracking for the last drops of oil in the ground is bad for the surrounding areas and just keeps us on an oil-based economy which is toxic. So, they place a proposal on the Google Super Vote site that says the following:

'A Proposal to abolish the practice known as Fracking'

'This legislation would abolish Fracking by all oil companies within the borders of the United States of America and any person or corporation that violated this law is subject to one BILLION DOLLARS in fines per day of each infraction thereof.'

So, the question I put to you, the reader is: Would you vote to PASS such legislation? Or would you vote it down?

I think that after reading the accompanying educational material on Fracking and how it is poisoning the water in the communities where it takes place, how there are now better ways of producing energy such as Solar, Wind, and even Nuclear, you may be easily convinced to vote to pass it.

Now, in our present form of government, whenever anyone of the Exceptionally Small Brain Trust might propose such a law to protect us all, his sworn duty, that individual is sent gobs of money in the form of campaign contributions by the Oil Companies. Then, these companies then swarm his office with their paid thugs, or lobbyists to intimidate this poor individual into dropping his proposal. They can and always win this intimidation because they have the money behind them to carry out their threats. They merely threaten to take this man's livelihood away, the loss of his job, by spending millions of dollars on smear campaigns against him on TV during his next election to his job.

This money to bribe him into accepting their point of view, which of course is to continue Fracking no matter how much damage they do - combined with the threat to destroy this person financially always does the trick and so real proposals that can do something good for society never has a chance in Congress due to this process that always occurs and is totally legal, so there is no danger for anyone to participate in this scam.

Therefore under the Google Super-Vote Super States of America, we might eventually also see a proposal like the following:

'A Proposal - To Abolish Lobbyists and all Lobbying Activity'

"From this point forward, anyone who pays any money or gives anything of value to any federal government official, shall be subject to ONE BILLION DOLLARS in fines and 100 years in prison without the possibility of parole.'

Now, would you support such legislation? My best guess is that the vast majority of Americans would vote YES to such a proposal and another major problem for American Democracy would be eliminated.

Some of the more astute of my readers would wonder how anyone would get elected under this proposal because they would have to finance their campaigns by themselves. And, I would say to that - this would be a better system. Let's have anyone running for office pay for their campaign costs out of their own pockets.

Because under the Google Super-Vote System, you really don't need any money to get yourself onto the ballot. I would suggest a certain number of FRIENDS who endorse your campaign would be sufficient to make it into the pool of candidates. From there, you might have to spend some money, but very little to get some attention on the Internet to have your ideas heard above the others.

However, people with the most endorsers would have an equal share in all of this attention because the Google Super-Vote algorithm gives priority to people who have the highest ratings on the Web. People who have the most THUMBS-UP on their ideas would outweigh any paid advertising by ten to one. So, again, this system is far superior in terms of fairness and opening the system to anyone than other system devised ever before in history. Yes, nothing devised by humans will be perfect and some of you are already finding flaws, although they may be minor ones, with my suggestions. I welcome better ideas from the public, because just like the Exceptionally Small Brain Trust of Congress, my brain has limitations almost as great.

I can go on and give you countless more examples of how useful the Google Super-Vote System can be used for the greater good and the eventual survival of our species. But, in future chapters I give you many more examples that come from the headlines of today. My greatest hope and desire is that you will continue with me in examining and evaluating this worthy suggestion given to us so generously by Google who I believe are standing by waiting for our decision to expand it into these areas and help us create the 'Super States of America' (Tm)

One more point about the Super States of America replacing the United States of America.

The Super-States of America, is such a valid notion that I have no doubt that this system would be emulated and eventually cloned by nearly every other country on the planet. Why? Because in order to compete in the global economy, every country would need to make decisions at the speed of light just as we would be making them, but they would also need to be making better decisions too and it would very quickly become apparent to every person now living that the Google Super-Vote system is far superior to anything they now suffer.

The Internet being the Greatest UNITER of all time, we would be in essence offering the rest of the world the same unifying and democratic benefits that we have enjoyed as the United States. Therefore, the next level that we must achieve in being the major benefactor to the world once again would come in the recognition of our status as 'The Super-States of America' (Tm)

And you may have noticed that I have TRADEMARKED this name but I will be gladly giving it away to the benefit of all Mankind. I am forced to Trademark it at this point only so that it can not be corrupted or co-opted by another person or group and made into something different.

Most importantly and I want to re-emphasize this as many times as I can. Remember too that the Google Super Vote system has within it the seeds of a completely new economic system for this country and as I have shown later the world. Because what it does is give us the path to gaining a greater and greater participation in the economic and political system by granting to any voter the ability to vote their shares. What I mean by this is that the Government, when it is setup as a For-Profit Corporation instead of the money-losing Non-Profit Organization that it is, grants to each of more stock shares in the country as a whole to people who produce greater and greater advances for society than people who do not produce these things.

In other words, what we want to consider mostly as we formalize plans for the Google Super Vote System is 'does it make sense for people who have created things that make our lives better deserve a little more say in the creation of our laws than someone who is just getting by?'

After careful consideration on this subject, it is my humble opinion that yes, people who contribute positive things that benefit society deserve more say in the political and economic system than someone who accomplishes very little or nothing in their lives.

We've already made this contention in the previous chapter so we won't belabor it here, but it is an essential ingredient in these proposals that we should also adapt our form of government so that these things can happen and happen on a daily basis with very little bureaucracy to enforce these changes. The Internet allows us to do all of the above with very little if any investment in terms of money.

In the rest of this book, I present you with a complete system that allows us to do all these things by the Incorporation of the United States of America so that we can evolve from he United States to the Super States of America where everyone gradually learns how to make the most of their time on this planet.

Why does the USA lose so much money? How can we fix that for all time? By making the USA a For Profit Corporation. Why does the government have so much power over us as individuals? Because the individual has no voice.

And I give you a 100% guaranteed method of reaching our goals by forcing Google to help us achieve the Real Democracy In America by putting this amazing and miraculous technology of the Internet to its highest and best use.

I implore all of my readers to join me in this quest by simply reading on and endorsing these ideas. Please share these completely new ideas with everyone you know.

CHAPTER Three: The Real Evolution

Before we can really appreciate the why's and wherefore's of incorporating our system of government and turning it into a more business-like entity, perhaps we should all look at the history of the evolution of government because when studied objectively, it is a fascinating tale indeed. The first government, during the time when we were known as cave dwellers, was probably a Patriarchy. A tribal leader, usually the strongest cave man would take up his club and declare himself to be the leader and much like a pack of wolves, a few other young cubs might challenge this self-proclaimed leadership of the biggest and the strongest and so probably this type of tribal leader was overthrown every few years as younger and stronger bucks came up against the leader and overthrew him in a bloody contest with knives and clubs.

Messy to say the least, but effective and brief revolutions like this made for a kind of order that the rest of the tribe could easily follow and obey. Then, after we became more agrarian and stopped chasing our food every day, around 10,000 years ago, with the development of proper housing or huts for the people who had now become farmers, roads would develop in between the most important huts and then even groups of these important huts where people who specialized in butchery, bakery and candle-stick making would be concentrated thus forming the earliest communities.

A system of governance for these early farmers and merchants would develop into what was later known as City-States where a tribal leader would bestow upon himself the Divine Right of Kings and Queens, wherein, they would rule with an iron hand with the aid of hired goon squads, we now know as Armies, Navies, Air Forces and Marines. Basically, this military power, kept the young bucks from overthrowing the tribal ruler for decades and sometimes even for generations, which lead to the dynastic powers that we know as the Egyptian Empire, the Greek Empire, the Persian Empire, the Chinese Empire, the Roman Empire etc. An empire being simply a

King who was bold enough to put into the laws of the land that his next of kin should become the next King or Queen upon his or her death.

The rule of Kings and Queens even extends to modern times where there are still Kings ruling over Saudi Arabia, Brunei, Great Britain (this power mostly symbolic) and indeed, my research tells me that there are a total of 31 countries out of about 277 nations on the Earth even today ruled by so-called Royalty.

Still more than 10% of the world's nations being ruled by folks who believe they are somehow stronger, better, wiser, more eligible to rule as the entire government in their region and their descendants to inherit this right for all eternity, no matter how good or bad they end up as a ruler. In a kingdom there is no accountability, no recourse by the people, no redress of grievances, no freedom of the press, freedom of speech or any other freedom we hold so dear in this country today and in many other countries.

The fact that these people rule with an iron fist over their countrymen does not escape most of us. If it were not for the military power that supports them, all of these people, or at least the vast majority of them, would be deposed almost instantly upon removal of the iron fist, their goon squad, armies, navies, secret police, etc.

And, in fact, if it were not for the American Revolution of 1776, probably many more positions of the world's populations would still be ruled in this heavy-handed way where the average citizen has no power to object to the rules of the road, no power to a fair trial when accused of a crime, no control even over his own person which is technically owned by the Sovereign Lord. Slavery is another word for it. We didn't care for that much in the British Colonies of three centuries ago and so we took to the streets, took on the British goon squads of the time, known as Redcoats, and as every school child all over the world now knows, won our freedom and independence.

This is how we go to where we are. Some of the bravest and brightest bulbs in the pack got the notion that we should all be equal under the law, that slavery was not a good thing and that there was no real Divine Right of Kings as the Kings had proclaimed for thousands of years.

Indeed, our founding fathers stated quite clearly and emphatically that if God was to get involved in human affairs, He would surely be on the side of the ordinary citizen, the family man or woman who was given life and that this life would belong to God and no one else. So, the Divine Right of Kings was out the window in 1776 for most of us and replaced by the right to be government being bestowed upon elected officials in what had come to be known as early as Ancient Greece as a "Democracy", a rule Of, By and For the People themselves and therefore a right that they themselves having bestowed could take back or alter in any way they might choose and at any time, without having to clear with anyone other than themselves.

This authority that Democracy gave to ordinary people is the basis of our government at least in America and a few other imitators in Europe and elsewhere and although flawed in many respects, it is still the best thing, in my humble opinion, that anyone has yet to create in the business of ruling over each other, creating the laws of the land and enforcing them and even giving a tribe of people their unique identity in the world as the fighters and defenders of freedom even unto the rest of the world. A great and noble cause, America is then, is it not?

And aren't we amongst the proudest of tribes to call ourselves Americans today? And isn't our system of government a proven best by the fact that millions of other oppressed people try to sneak in here every day? Is there any reason to question the continued existence of such a great and noble cause? I think not. However, it is not done.

Our democracy is only a half-way house in the quest for real democracy, isn't it? The founding fathers who created our democracy were afraid to some extent of the granting of too much power to the people too fast, so accustomed they were to living under the rule of kings. It seemed almost unnatural that ordinary people would have as much power as they themselves, since they, our founding fathers owned large tracts of lands, some of them as big as states are today. And, nearly all of them owned slaves. Thomas Jefferson freed his slaves as soon as he started to think about the great notions that he and his friends penned into the basic documents of our Constitution.

John Adams, George Washington, James Madison, Alexander Hamilton, the signers of our basic framework of government all owned slaves, but eventually gave them their freedom, after realizing the dichotomy, the cognitive dissonance of proclaiming freedom to all white men, they had forgotten for a short while that even black men deserved freedom too under their own logic. Having nowhere else to go, most of these early freed slaves stayed on to work for their masters, but this time being given a wage, a few pennies per day and a roof over their heads and free medical care, such as it was.

However, our own basic framework, the United States Constitution, the basic law we live under today, made slavery itself legal because they knew that their friends who owned large estates and farms relied on those slaves for their own livelihood and they simply could not imagine a better way to get the crops to market in an efficient yet humanistic manner. Slavery was not outlawed until the 13th Amendment in 1865 and passed with the aid of President Abraham Lincoln, still today one of our greatest Presidents, because he saw to the completion of the list of freedoms that was guaranteed to us in a free and democratic society.

NOW THIS IS A MAJOR POINT I AM MAKING HERE.

The evolution of Government really has stopped there. Since 1865, our Constitution really hasn't been improved other than to give women the right to vote in the 1920's. BUT NEITHER WHITE PERSON OR BLACK, MALES or FEMALES, YOUNG OR OLD have gained any more rights or basic freedoms truly since that time, more than a century ago. We still have an unfinished democracy because also created by our Constitution besides legalized slavery was the manner in which we elect our representatives in Congress and how they represent us based on population, the House of Representatives, and apportioned by states, in the United States Senate.

The average citizen's interests, it was stated and still pertains today would be safeguarded by these elected United States Representatives and Senators and the will of the people, or at least the vast majority of us expressed by these same people and put down and codified into the laws of the land by these same people given their authority to do so by US, We the People.

For a couple hundred years, this system has served us well enough. However, recent events suggest to many of us that we are no longer served by these same elected representatives nor the system that made them thus, giving them a new kind of Divine Right of Power. Kings and Queens it seems have been replaced by pompous and arrogant white men in business suits who are elected to office after months spoon-feeding us quaint little sound bites to help us think of them as good folks just like us. But, as soon s they are in office they change their spots and start listening to the lobbyists more than the people who elected them to office.

Even descendants of these same rulers have claimed their rights to these same offices. I love the Kennedy family, but who would argue that they are not a dynasty of power and rule over us? Al Gore, the son of a Senator almost made it to President of the Untied States and indeed is a good person. Largely because of his work for the environment, I like Al Gore very much, but who would argue that someone else outside his family would have done as good a job? George W. Bush, the son of a Director of the CIA who went on to become President felt that his claim to the White House was a Divine Right and who would argue that anyone else could have done a better job from 2000 to 2008?

Getting elected to office has itself come to be a big business. Campaigns for these same offices now run into the HUNDREDS OF MILLIONS OF DOLLARS, which few of us can afford. So, people have emerged from the shadows who know where large pots of money are and they beg the support of these people and entities and spend it all on so much advertising and marketing that most of us get fooled every four years into thinking that this time, we found someone who will represent us.

Indeed, each and every candidate uses that vaunted and clichéd phrase to help convince us it is true, when the truth is that they will leave these offices as multi-millionaires, sometimes even billionaires and to the great detriment of our laws, policies and rules that we are forced to endure in our daily lives. If you want proof of this total lack of representation, you only have to read the laws that they have enacted over the last fifty years. Almost none of them reflect the true interests of the average citizen, no matter what state or region they are from.

Everyone should agree that Congress, for example has the mission of regulating Wall Street, but as Bernie Sanders (I) from Vermont said the other day, "Nowadays, it's the other way around. Wall Street regulates Congress."

There are a few notable exceptions. Social Security is one of this country's greatest achievements, but that set of laws were passed during World War II under Franklin D. Roosevelt, a man who really was a man of the people and probably the last one of that type. Even though from a wealthy family, he felt that the little guy was not getting an even break and said so many times in many ways and most of our modern laws that truly represent the needs of the people have their origins in this one great man.

Most Presidents and most of Congress have busied themselves reversing these great advancements in civilization. George W. AMBUSH even being so bold as to start the privatization of our great Retirement plans and making them subject to the whims of the stock market. Later machinations by Bush would teach us why he wanted to do this. The transfer of our payroll taxes into Wall Street Brokerage firms where they would have managed our accounts for us would have made them TRILLIONS OF DOLLARS in fees and commissions and their track record such as it is, probably to no great advantage to our retirement incomes at all and more likely to the great trimming of our benefits.

And, as far as the White House goes, there is no mention in the Constitution that the President shall have the right to make war on any foreign nation. Yet, Lyndon Johnson did it. Richard Nixon did it. George W. AMBUSH did it and so did his father. So, truly what we have as far as National In-Security is concerned is a ONE-MAN RULE.

This is not exactly what I would call democracy in action and so in a way, we have evolved full circle back to the Divine Right of Kings and Queens when our founding fathers gave us the rule of the ordinary citizen over ourselves, known as a "Democracy". The fact that they labeled the first version of America as a Republic matters not because the Republic for which we all pledge our allegiance as school children was based on the principles of Democratic rule and the promise of more advanced features of democracy have been written in stone and in blood into all of our actions in amending the Constitution up to this day.

So, our Constitution is a living and evolving document set up to be a living and evolving document wherein We The People have every right and even a duty to change and adapt at our will. If this were not true, slavery would still be legal and acceptable today, women would still be second class citizens and the ordinary worker in this country would have no rights, we would have no middle class and we would all be working in some way, shape or fashion for our lords and masters.

Instead, we have had the ability over the years to extend our rights and privileges and we have done so under this limited form of democracy bringing us ever closer and closer to the dream of a full expression of democracy and democratic principles. Where you give freedom a chance to grow, wherever you plant the seed of freedom and equality and love of country, this seed will take root and it will grow into a great tree of life.

The founding fathers understood this great natural principle and they planted that seed, but the growth of the tree is under attack from the pesticides of modern forms of the Divine Right of Kings and Queens who want to rule over us and rule over us forever. Something has to give. Or else we are all doomed to repeat history over and over where the oppressed eventually get angry enough to overthrow their oppressors and it's usually not pretty and it can lead to even worse state of affairs.

We must be careful and ever vigilant to not make this great mistake of history and trust those who advocate the violent overthrow of our oppressors because in this case, at this point in history, our oppressors are us. We have done this to ourselves by the simple act of omission. Through our apathy, the forces of evil have taken their power over us. By simply turning from apathy to activism and choice, we can move this great country back into the proper tradition of more freedom, more democracy, more optimism and success.

It seems to me, however, that these choices that we make in the near future must include a basic and fundamental change to the system itself. Hiring another one of these cronies to do our bidding is not enough. We have suffered such a long string of disappointments that it is now clear that We the People must take a closer and stronger hold of the reins.

The only way to do that is to make our own political and economic system more responsive and more agile in bringing about the most benefit to the most people most of the time. This is our only hope. The greatest debates in politics for the last century or so has been the great debate about Socialism vs. Capitalism. There are plus sides to each system of government of course. The positive side of Capitalism is that it allows the individual to succeed or fail in life based on his or her own merits and work activities. The negative side of Capitalism is that it provides for a Boom or Bust type economy.

And boy are we in one of the worst Busts in history at the moment. Sadly it could have all been avoided too, millions of people might not have lost their homes, thousands of unnecessary deaths could have been prevented except for the lack of leadership and morality from those in Charge.

In the last century or so, we've had to major Booms and two major Busts, the last one having started during the Bush Administration for reasons we explain in a later chapter on the excesses of Power. But, this Boom and Bust cycle of Capitalism has another negative side effect in that these cycles produce a greater and greater gap between the richest strata of society and the poorest.

Today, for example, wealthiest amongst us are able to afford dozens of homes all over the world, private jets, a caviar and champagne lifestyle with little worries about their future. The poorest segment of our society, by far the largest segment, and this rift wouldn't be so bad if it were reversed with many times more people in the wealthy category of society than in the poorest strata, but alas it is not reversed.

The lowest strata of our society is combined from vast masses of us who are struggling to feed our children and make the payments on our houses or apartments and the fear of being jobless and homeless is currently rampant all across the land because the vast majority of us don't get the chances to score big in business, the stock market, real estate, etc. and we run out of time.

We get older and slower, or we get sick and can't work as hard as we once could. So, the negative side of pure Capitalism is that people are treated like cattle and are abused by the Capitalists who take advantage of their poor bargaining skills and make profits from the daily labors of the poorest of us without providing us with any real safety nets or any real future or even hope for the future.

Of course, we don't enjoy a pure Capitalistic state any more. Today, we are somewhere in between pure Socialism and pure Capitalism because we provide many safety nets for our poorest classes. However, there are now more safety nets for this lower segments that the upper segments can little afford to keep it going in the black, so we have been forced to borrow from the future generations of rich and poor to support the massive social programs of today. And to such an extent now that we are inevitably headed for bankruptcy, if we're not already there. Being propped up artificially by China, a combination itself of Communism and Capitalism, and other countries, this is not a good thing for our future freedoms and traditions.

The plus side of Socialism is that there are such safety nets in place that everyone is guaranteed something to eat and a place to stay along with completely free medical care. The power of the economic decision-making to sustain such a huge cost on society is place in the hands of a small bureaucracy, who have little incentive to get things right, being that they can never be removed from office. There are no freedoms of speech or of the press, so if anyone wants to make a complaint or even offer up a suggestion, this citizen can find himself imprisoned or shot in the head without a trial, as we have seen in China currently and in the Soviet Union in the recent past.

The People being the greatest force of change no matter how much you oppress them, this complete system of Socialism has either collapsed all over the world wherever it has been applied such as in the Soviet Union, East Germany, Poland, Eastern Europe, soon Cuba, etc. or it has adapted and changed to more modern versions of Socialism such as in China where the allow the people to make the basic decisions about where to work and so forth, but they also limit free speech and there is no freedom of the press or judicial freedom and you can still be shot in the head for objecting to any of this.

However, it should be noted, and it certainly has been noted by billions in China and around the world that it is the engine of Freedom of Choice and Capitalism that has made China the greatest economic power in the world, recently surpassing that role of the United States. The Chinese economy is exploding at around 10% per year, something unheard of in the West, solely because the Chinese Communist Party has loosened their Maoist grip on society and let them work for their own personal successes.

This most basic need to succeed and provide some of the modern goods and luxuries of today's society is what spurs most of us on to create and work hard in society, providing jobs for other people and thus stimulating the revenues of the state and making their country rich in terms of money, economic growth and power, and especially in personal achievement.

These two simple economic factors always seem to go hand in hand in creating the best economies the world has ever known. The key then, it seems to me is to continue this trend toward combining the best of both political and economic models. If we incorporate our government, we use the best part of Capitalism, the Corporate model of growth, change, job creation, profit making, business ethics, governance, etc.

And, by incorporating, we also have the chance to allow everyone to share in the wealth, the equity that is created by society acting as a whole and pulling in the same direction that Socialism promises, without any of the negative sides of each system used in and of itself. So, the best of both systems are struggling now to maintain some kind of equilibrium. But, the next step eludes us all. Currently our leaders in government and business are squabbling amongst themselves and in public over every little detail.

The current debate is raging around how to afford Health Care for everyone in this country and how to regulate the banks, reverse the massive Bonuses that the financial corps are paying to all the cronies, the same people who acted so unethically and so recklessly to cause the pain and suffering now felt all over the world and so that the Second Great Depression doesn't continue for much longer or to prevent a third. These squabbles over minor petty details about how to run a nation, how to rebuild the economy, how to share in the equity of society is a squabble that obscures the greater issue: How to bring about real changes, real changes that everyone can appreciate and enjoy and that will last into the far off future of Humanity?

The evolution of business into the modern day corporation and the evolution of the modern day form of government can and must now merge and unite to bring us one clean and simple over arching system of governance that could not be 'Gamed' as the modern politicians have 'gamed' the system that exists today. In this one simple and graceful motion to a more common sense approach to managing the way we do business in this country and the way we control our society, we accomplish the instant hybridization of both of the greatest economic philosophies in the history of Mankind.

In this way, we combine the best of both worlds and rid ourselves of the negative sides of both as well, maximizing the best and most positive sides of both systems. We can have it all. We can have nearly everyone become wealthy and prosperous and healthy and rested and relieved of the stresses of life. And, we can have a booming economy, employing our greatest talents, utilizing all of our best ideas, most creative works, hard work and due diligence nearly one hundred percent of the time because everyone would be a shareholder in the total economic output.

We still have the right to fail because if we all goof off and take too many vacations or forget how the system is designed or try to abuse it, like anything else created by humans, it will also fail, and we will not participate in the profits and we will become poorer for it, but it will be ALL OF US WHO FAIL TOGETHER, from TOP TO BOTTOM, instead of just the poorest of us failing to thrive in these circumstances and that is the basic difference that we can have if we want it. Tremendous success for everyone, if we want it. Or a shared experience of losses if we do not work together and in harmony.

I leave it to future generations to decide which way they want it to go? But until we achieve a system where everyone shares equally in the successes and failures of our society as a whole, there can be no Real Democracy, there can be no really favorable ultimate destiny of Mankind, because if we do not improve our system of making these kinds of decisions we will simply continue to destroy our planet, piece by piece, as we are now doing under the present systems of uncontrolled, mismanaged and unregulated human greed, and then what? Where do we go from there?

In the next chapter, we'll look at the Evolution of the best business model ever invented and hopefully the reader will agree that it may be time to hybridize the best form of government to yet evolve with the best and most highly evolved form of business for the purpose of achieving the greatest good in the world as a whole and this nation in particular.

CHAPTER FOUR: The Incorporation of the USA

Business in cave man times was of course extremely basic as people would trade what they had for what they needed. The barter system, still in use today would allow one cave man to hunt down a deer or a wild boar and then trade the skin for say a hunting knife or weapon, or some meat for a bottle of beer. This system of trading lasted until, you guessed it, we evolved into creatures capable of settling down out of the caves and into the small villages and towns that would later become cities and states.

While living in these small rural communities, one butcher or baker or candle-stick maker would be so successful at his or her craft that they had all the meat they wanted in trade for their goods or had an overstock of animal skins, having the ability to only wear one fur at a time, or eat just a small portion of meat at a time. The surplus they might receive for their candles or baked goods or for their meat would lead to a spoilage or pilferage of their stockpiles that represented the earliest forms of equity or money.

Eventually someone would carve out a small stone to represent money and everyone in the village would agree that one stone with a hole in the middle would be equal in value to one deer skin, or one pound of meat. Then, the person who made this money for the tribe would eventually find himself with too much of this commodity too and the modern bank was created to store all the extra money in the community in a safe place where pilferage would be discouraged.

Now, somebody would come along who was very good at counting all this money. He would become an accountant, or bean counter as they are known today and the modern economic system would be formed around the counting, hoarding and control of the money. The village accountant or lawyer, whatever they were called in those days, would have an unusual amount of influence over the rest of the tribe as he would be a controller of the currency and would make simple investments in one person's small business over another.

Perhaps the village was starting to enjoy someone's pastries more than others and the idea of investing in that person would be the next major step in the direction of capitalism. During Roman times, the idea of a corporation was created. The word corporation stems from the Latin word 'Corpus' or 'Body' and today the corporation's legal status is the same as any other human body and even has the status of being alive or dead under the law.

In Roman times, these artificial 'bodies' were put in place to establish some charitable purpose. Then, over the centuries other more modern states chartered a corporation as a Royal Charter and this tradition is still alive today in some modern kingdoms. Then in the mid nineteenth century the British Parliament enacted the Joint Stock Companies Act of 1844 whereupon some of the earliest rules of common incorporation came into being and which we now rely on even today. This government action allowed individuals for the first time could follow certain procedures to become known as a private corporation, a separate legal body.

This Act of Parliament is probably the greatest single bit of legislation it has ever performed as a governmental decree since it established the longest running global prosperity that is still ongoing today. Despite our frequent recessions and even Great Depressions the corporation allows for more people to be gainfully employed than any other business model so far. From these humble notions about business models corporations have evolved from a very basic model to what it is today, the staunchest supporting structure of our modern economy.

In medieval Europe, churches became incorporated, as did some local governments in the cities that were really what we would call countries today. London would incorporate at this time because it was realized that the corporation would survive longer than the lives of any particular member, existing in perpetuity. The oldest commercial corporation in the world, basically a group of copper miners in Sweden received a corporate charter from King Magnus II in 1347. A century later many European nations chartered corporations to lead colonial ventures such as the Dutch East India Company and the Hudson's Bay Company.

The Dutch East India company became practically a nation with their own armies and navies patrolling the world solely for the benefit of the corporation and doing pretty much whatever they pleased. This one corporation would almost by itself lead to the greatest social change in history by enslaving millions of natives wherever they could be found and sending them to Europe and then America to work in indentured servitude, a polite word for slavery. Not exactly a good example of corporate governance that we will want to emulate today.

In 1819, the U.S. Supreme Court granted corporate rights not previously recognized. Corporations were deemed "inviolable" and not subject to arbitrary amendment or abolition by state governments. The corporation became an "artificial person" and under the law would now enjoy both individuality and immortality, something not yet granted to the truly living amongst us.

During this time, England would introduce the notion of Limited Liability to the corporate persona. And in the 20th century, and as recently as the 1980's, large state corporations would go private by the selling of the corporate assets to private investors while at the same time, world governments have acted in unison to make private corporate regulations by the state become gradually less and less restricting to those individuals, thus reducing the heavy burden of bureaucracy on corporate governance and political control, a move toward the "Laissez Faire" philosophy of days gone by.

Since the 1980's we have generally seen the conglomeration, the combining of many large corporations into a conglomerate of them all with the biggest most powerful corporations swallowing up the smaller ones and becomes what is known now as the Multi-Nationals and what I would call the business world emulating the Natural World in a new form of Darwinism, or the Survival of the Fittest.

To Summarize:

The evolution of government and the evolution of business have followed along in parallel paths. The evolution of business follows right along in the footsteps of government progresses and mutations as outlined above. Just as government became the playing field for the God-appointed kings and queens, business has evolved into the playing field for the loftiest of business people, now paid like Royalty with the notable exception that in the American model of business and other European nations, even the average Joe can get involved and make his fortune.

This has become known all around the world as the 'American Dream', a notion, greatly admired and emulated all over the world where anyone with a good idea and lots of hard work can make a huge shining success of himself. The most common ways that modern fortunes are made is to incorporate and enough issue stock to the founding principles that they will become billionaires, or at least millionaires if and when the stock becomes popular and is picked up as a good investment by the investment public on Wall Street.

These later stock investors would inevitably bid up the value of these stock shares in the corporation to increase the value of the initial shares owned by the founding principles, thus making them wealthy beyond their wildest dreams. Examples of this modern path to wealth are the notable Bill Gates, who was smart enough and lucky enough to court IBM just as they were looking for an operating system for their new invention, the personal computer.

Warren Buffet, who made his name by simply becoming a good stock trader and which propelled him to becoming one of the richest men in the world. Sam Walton, who started out with a small retail store in Arkansas and built it into Wall-Mart, the largest chain store in the world and making him one of the richest men in the world. The list goes on and on.

Donald Trump is on that list having made his billions in Real Estate. And, even George W. Bush having made his fortune by simply being the son of an influential Republican was given participation in several corporations and owning some thousands of shares sufficient to making him wealthy and then even attaining the most powerful office in the world largely from the same concentrated influence and money.

And without a corporate governance model, we will continue to hire the wrong people for the job. Our current system is over-influenced by two major political parties, the so-called Democratic Party and the aptly named, Republican Party, for the 200 year old guard is what this nation was founded on, the idea of a Republic. The Roman Empire called itself a Republic too. So, the name is a good one that denotes a nod toward democracy, but a Dynastic Empire at the root of everything, thus giving the lie to any claims to real democracy.

The evolution of the business model has brought us to the present day where the differences between corporate executives and government officials is dimmed and obscured. There really is no difference in the hen house between the chickens and the fox. Both of them are after the same thing, personal gratification and that means money, power, prestige or all three for themselves with total disregard for the proper disposition of their duties and responsibilities.

What is the difference after all between the Chief Executives in Enron with the Bush family? Really none. Both of them fraudulently misrepresented themselves and defrauded their shareholders, the people out of billions if not trillions of dollars. But as we have seen the corporation was designed and has evolved into a living being with the same protection under the law as any other living citizen.

The protections that we as living citizens are guaranteed under the Constitution almost require the same kind of bylaws and protections of limited liability, total responsibility for one's assumed duties as an officer of the corporation and the ability to survive for decades even after the death of the founding principles. This is just the beginning of the list of benefits this author sees by the incorporation of the State. What we may someday refer to as 'Pop Corporatism' to replace outright unregulated Capitalism.

CHAPTER FIVE – The Bylaws of the Corporation America 2.0, Inc.

So, today, we must begin to think about the bylaws of our National Government as a corporate entity and they should have as their core the following basic principles. These are not the complete list of bylaws as I will welcome the suggestions of my readers for many things that I could not have considered. The following should serve only as a starting point.

Some may not be comprehensible to the general public, but these are what I would call the most likely to be acceptable to all of us. I hope it is just the foundation of what will eventually evolve. There are many more bylaws that I would not be able to conjure up on my own but that others may wish to add. We invite more suggestions for these ByLaws, the basic We invite more suggestions for these ByLaws, the basic foundation of the new nation at: http://www.america2inc.com/bylaws.htm The Bylaws of America 2.0, Inc

1. The National Budget of America 2.0, Inc. shall always be in balance, i.e., with expenditures never exceeding revenues. Any elected leader who conspires to spend more than what the corporation of America takes in from revenues shall be impeached and removed from office through the use of the National Ballot Measure mechanism – also a bylaw of the Corporation.

1. A. The Government may NOT approve a federal budget that is not in balance, except during times of a national emergency such as War or major natural disasters. In any year where the budget is not in perfect balance, the legislators of both houses shall have all of the salaries and benefits withheld in an escrow account that they are not authorized to use, until such times as the budget is in balance in which all monies owed shall be paid out.

2. The government of America 2.0, Inc. shall be operated on the principles of honest and ethical business governance as set forth in corporate business law and shall abide by all common accounting principles as set forth in United States Legal Code, all encompassing.

3. The government of America 2.0, Inc. shall be accountable to the shareholders and shall issue stock to the citizens of the United States as apportioned in a formula devised by Congress and as amended by Congress in such manner that stock ownership will be used for the purpose of funding all social programs that the citizens may require for their health, education and welfare and which upon in a National Ballot Measure. Full disclosure and accountability shall be required in all governmental proceedings.

4. Any new taxation by the Government of the people directly or indirectly must be put forth for approval by the people in the form of a National Referendum or National Ballot Measures. No, increase in taxation may be approved with less than a Three-Fourths (75%) Majority Vote by the People. Congress may decrease personal taxes at any time without a Ballot Measure.

5. Any new policies or programs conceived by Congress must be paid for from ongoing revenues or new revenues thus approved by the People.

6. No Government employee can be secure in their position and can be removed by the people for cause at any time, should the people feel it necessary to remove any person from office for any reason under an open Impeachment process that shall be called with a Petition by the voters signed by more than 50% of the voters. An impeachment hearing must then be held for the government employee in question and the decision shall be rendered by a panel of citizens picked at random by the Executive Branch. Once impeached a government employee is barred from any federal posting of any kind for the duration of their life.

7. No Government employee may conspire to unravel any of these bylaws, which may be amended only by Congress, and only with a 75% majority or by a two-thirds majority of the Voters in a National Ballot Measure.

8. National Ballot Measures must be held at any time that there is a General Federal Election and popular measures can originate from the people or from Congress upon the meeting of certain minimum criteria for the ballot as set forth by the Federal Election Commission. Or use Google Super-Vote to reach a plurality, gets to the top of that heap.

9. Making Lobbying (A form of Bribery) the highest crime in the land. No Federal Employee may accept gifts of cash or any products or services of any significant value or benefit to themselves or their friends and family. Penalty for violation this bylaw is the immediate removal of the employee in question as well as the confiscation of all benefits received and deposited into the Federal Treasury. The giver of the gifts is also subject to a $100,000 Fine and no less than a ten year sentence in prison upon conviction of such violation.

10. The federal government must be operated on a business like manner under long-held traditions of good business principles, ethics, accountability, etc. This means that expenditures must not exceed revenues in each fiscal year WHICH WILL BE MAINTAINED by each agency in the government striving for a profit in any given fiscal year.

11. In any years that total revenues received do not equal total expenditures then, an equal amount of such deficit must be deducted from the payroll of the government employees in order to meet the deficit.

12. If the deficit still exists after deductions of federal payroll to balance, then no salaries must be paid until such revenues can be raised to equal expenditures or spending is cut to balance out total revenues received. This rule does not apply in times of war or national emergency. War and National Emergencies can exist for

purposes of ByLaw number 10, only as declared by Congress and supported by a vote of no less than a two thirds majority in Congress.

13. Any military action requiring any enlisted soldiers of the United States Armed Forces, taken by the Executive Branch, must be ratified by Congress with a minimum Two Thirds majority within 30 days of the start of said executive military action or troops come home.

If any employee shall be removed from their office by a National Ballot Impeachment, they shall not be eligible to return to employment by the government corporation for the rest of their lives.

13. Foreign Aid projects shall be given only upon the Approval of the Voters in a National Ballot Measure and only after a minimum 75% Majority.

14. No Ballot Measure may pass and become law, or no law may be abolished or amended without at least a minimum of a Two Thirds Majority.

15. The method of raising taxes on the people and the amount of the taxable amounts of income or equity shall be abridged or vetoed at any time during any National Ballot. However, any Ballot Measure that increases or decreases government revenues by greater than 1% must have a waiting period of at least 1 year for discussion and debate and another 2 years between the date such change is enacted by the National Ballot Measures and the date that it can take effect thus giving government agencies time to plan and react to changing revenue expectations.

15 A. Stock in the United States of America, Inc. must be distributed to the people in such manner that will ensure fairness amongst all workers regardless of income or job description. Consideration must also be given to larger contributions to society as a whole such as inventions, successful completion of goals and expectations by key executives, productivity by cooperation and added education or training and experience etc. A formula must be

devised that can also be altered from time to time to meet changing economic climates. Alterations in the formula for Stock Distribution can only be made by ballot measures having a two thirds majority or by Congress but only after a Three-Fourths majority in both houses.

15 – B. The goal for the formula for stock distribution for workers should always be to have the largest possible number of workers reach retirement age with enough equity in their country to ensure a comfortable and dignified retirement which includes enough to satisfy a minimum standard of living in America plus sufficient health care to prevent any loss of their dwelling.

16. Anyone who wants a job in America 2. Inc. has the right to work as long as he or she is a citizen in good standing. A citizen of the United States of America 2.0, Inc. is any person born within the boundaries of this nation or has become a naturalized citizen through the formal process of Immigration and Naturalization as prescribed by law. Anyone who enters this country illegally is not entitled to anything, but may apply for Naturalization within the specifications of the law and when openings exist in the labor force of this nation, they may be approved for inclusion into citizenship after the application process has been approved and Stock Ownership in America 2.0, Inc. shall begin at the entry level.

17. All social benefits that are approved by Congress or the Voters directly must be paid for by the Stock Accumulation of each citizen. All labor, all endeavor of any kind, including but not limited to creative works of art and entertainment, transporting others, feeding others, working for others or for society in any service including housework has value for society and must also be eligible for Stock Ownership in America 2.0, Inc. under equal weight as any other job or profession.

17 - A In other words, stock ownership must not be weighted in terms of the status or prestige of the type of work that is done. A doctor or lawyer does not vest in any more stock equity in this country than someone who picks our fruits and vegetables.

We all require all forms of service at various stages in our lives. This does not mean that Doctors or Lawyers may not earn more money in the form of Salary and bonuses. It only means that we are all stock holders in America at the same rate of service. Individual success as measured by one's wealth, in other words is now and always should be a measure of one's hard work and success and ideas and imagination and creativity in our preferred line of work. If we did not reward the most creative and hard-working people in our society more than others, the entire fabric of the economy would break down.

However, one's wealth in terms of how lucky a person is in their lives compared to others, does not adjust the rights of one person over another in the ownership or equity of the nation as a whole because we are all necessary cogs in the wheels of society. We are all equal in the eyes of our Creator. This is the basic foundation of our country and this is what makes us great.

Equality of the individual must no longer and never more be confused with the inequality of our financial success. I believe strongly that this should be included in these by-laws for this reason. It seems to me that this inequality of human value was the main reason for ALL our financial collapses in the past and is remedied here.

(Many new and even more productive By-Laws will be proposed by myself and we welcome more suggestions by our readers.

To SUGGEST a new by-law to America 2.0, Inc. or any other suggestion for this boo, please send an email to: america2inc@gmail.com   Put the word "By-Law-Suggestion" in the subject of your email. There are undoubtedly many more BY-LAWS of our new Corporate Government that YOU can conceive that may be far more effective and useful than mine. We need to discuss them all at length at some point and this is the first order of business before we run off half-cocked to do something as radical as changing our form of government to this degree.

THE OVER-RIDING PRINCIPLE of the By-Laws of the Federal Corporation is that they MUST work to give the Shareholders, that's you and me, baby, the right to remove officers of the corporation at any time. The right to openness and honesty in all government workers and above all, the ability to track our money in ways that PAY OFF BIG TIME and NEVER LOSE our investments, our contributions to the economy in our only real assets, our time and energy.

We must be able to control their spending in a very timely manner before they spend us into ruin, before they are forced to raise our taxes and/or reduce our standard of living. The By-Laws must always reflect the ethics of sound business acumen and management and the return to the Shareholders a constantly growing and enduring dividend that is worth working and dying for, because this is what we do. We work and die for our country and this should be enough for us all to prosper, not just the lucky ones at the TOP.

CHAPTER SIX: The Balance Sheet of The United States Inc.

So, let's get to the BOTTOM LINE.

The rewards of Corporatism are all dependent on the growth of the American economy. As incentives for Americans to work harder and smarter and continue to contribute to society throughout their lives, rewards are vested in the form of an increasing stock distribution paid out at the various stages of one's life, and in proportion to the value of the individual's contributions.

The measure of success for all participants in the corporation comes from the reporting to the citizens from time to time in quarterly reports to all shareholders and the biggest metric would be hopefully a steady increase in the assets of the country in the form of a national corporate Profit and Loss Statement, a picture of profitability over a period of time and the Balance Sheet, a snap shot of the financial health of any organization at any specific point in time.

The Balance Sheet of any corporation is based in the long run on the Profits and Losses of that corporation over time. Later in this chapter, we will study the profit potential of the Corporation of the United States of America. For now, we must examine where we are – The Balance Sheet of our Country as of this date and time, as written, October of 2008. When you think about the Value of the United States of America and the value of the individual shares in our great nation, we must now be prepared for the shock of our lives.

The net worth of our nation is right actually LESS THAN ZERO. That's right. If we take the thousands-years-old Accounting formula of: Assets – Liabilities = Net Worth We come up with the following sobering results. For the purposes of this EVALUATION of how much we're worth as a nation, first let's start totaling up our National Assets.

All data is based on the data reported by the Federal Reserve, the National Association of Realtors, and Dun and Bradstreet as of Oct. 7, 2008. (In our current economic situation, it is safe to assume that these net asset values will decrease over the next few years and net liabilities will increase from this date.) The Assets of this country are the sum total of all the CORPORATE WEALTH and all the PRIVATE WEALTH.

At the present time, there are approximately 14 million corporations and small businesses headquartered in the United States. The average net worth of all the small businesses and corporations in this country is approximately, $425,000. That's just the average Net Worth of a corporation in the USA. Obviously many corporations are worth billions and many others are basically worthless, so the average is the sum total of all Net Worth on the Balance Sheets of all Corporations divided by the number of corporations and it comes to $925,000 and change.

(This is calculated by taking the value of all Corporate Assets and then deducting all Corporate Debt.) This is based on the actual BOOK VALUE of all business assets. We ignored such intangibles as Goodwill and Stock Values, since stock values are inflated at 20 to 40 times the Earnings of most publicly traded corporations. And, we rounded up. Therefore, the Total Net Worth of all Public and Private Corporate assets is 9 Trillion, 950 Billion Dollars or let's just use the abbreviation of 5.96 Trillion and let's round up this time to 10 TRILLION DOLLARS, since we may be slightly under valuing things like corporate Real Estate holdings, foreign investment and so forth.

So, our ASSETS as a NATION are pegged at approximately TEN TRILLION DOLLARS in real BOOK VALUE, things that we can see and SPEND and confiscate in a Bankruptcy. This is the only real measure of value as any creditor will tell you. When a Bank Loans you money on your mortgage, they always send out an appraiser to look at your house and he makes his best estimate of what your house is worth if the bank had to take it from you in a foreclosure.

That's the REAL VALUE of your home and that is what we must always base our values on when thinking in terms of SHAREHOLDERS VALUE. Next, we must get a total value of all PRIVATE SECTOR ASSETS, this would be the total of the value of all the Private Real Estate, your personal homes and investment homes, the sum total of all your savings accounts and all of your stock market portfolios, the value of your cars, furniture, clothing and jewelry in America. There are approximately 100 Million Single Family Homes in America and the average value today, as we write this book is around $200,000.

That makes the Total Value of all homes in America at approximately TWENTY TRILLION DOLLARS. However over 50% of all the homes in America are mortgaged to almost their full value and in some cases such as foreclosure and defaulted mortgages, the owners owe more than the value of their homes. That means we can conservatively cut the TOTAL ASSET VALUE of all homes in America to around TEN TRILLION DOLLARS in Book Value.

Bank Accounts, Savings Accounts, Stock Retirement Funds of all individuals in America today total another Ten Trillion Dollars approximate and rounded up. Total Loans Outstanding for personal consumer consumption such as cars, boats furniture, clothing, etc. is approximately 5 TRILLION DOLLARS and this was rounded down. Therefore NET ASSET VALUE of all personal households, excluding their homes is around 5 Trillion Dollars as of the writing of this book.

So, now we have all our Data and can calculate by our formula the Net Worth of the United States if it were a corporation today. NET ASSETS: Business Assets: 10 Trillion Dollars Personal Assets: 5 Trillion Dollars Social Security Net Present Value 1 Trillion (Rounded up from 940 Billion) NET LIABILITIES: National Debt 12.5 Trillion Dollars (This doesn't take into account the ONE TRILLION DOLLARS being spent this year to SUPPORT THE ECONOMY, more on the way and the money that is PROMISED in Social Security, Medicare, etc.) NET WORTH: (16 Trillion in Assets – 16 Trillion in National Debt.) Oops, no help there.

Next, let's calculate the Value of our Shares as of Today: First we must assume that most American workers in this country would have earned at a minimum in their 30's and 40's at least 10,000 Shares of Stock in America if Stock were issued today. This would represent an equity position that we can now calculate. There are approximately 200 Million People in the United States over the age of 18. Therefore, the total number of shares outstanding should be set at: 2,000,000,000,000 (2 Trillion Shares Outstanding)

So, here's the BOTTOM LINE. THIS NATION'S CURRENT VALUE A MEASLY $1.75 PER SHARE For a country that was once and could be again the WORLD'S MOST SUCCESSFUL and POWERFUL economy? (Do we call this mismanagement or theft?) A share of stock in the richest country in the world should be around ONE THOUSAND DOLLARS PER SHARE. Shares of Google are currently around $500 Per Share and were on their way to $1,000 Per Share before the Bush Depression set in.

Surely the United States of America, as a corporation should be worth more than GOOGLE, as useful as Google is, it's not as useful to the world as America herself, is it? Think about that for a moment. MacDonald's Corporation has a current value per share of $57 Per Share. Apple Computer Corporation has a value of around $500 per share and has been as low as $10 per share and as high as $200 Per Share. IBM shares are valued today at around $85 Per Share and has sold as high as $130 Per Share this year . Bank of America is selling at around $8.00 Per Share and has sold as high as $50 per share recently.

Google, one of the most excellent and highly regarded corporations in the history of corporations is currently selling for approximately $350 Per Share but that is during one of the worst market downturns in history, OCT of 2008. Previously in the same year Google was selling for around $700 per share and many analysts believed it was headed for $1,000 Per Share. The price of gold is currently around $1,500 Per Ounce. It would seem to the casual observer that shares in the United States of America should be selling at a MINIMUM at least as much as the shares of one of the finest High-Tech corporations in America, such as Google, or for at least the price of ONE OUNCE of GOLD. However, this price of $2,10 per share illustrates just how badly our government, our nation has been mis-managed over the last several decades by a bunch of scoundrels claiming to be "Fiscal Conservatives".

In reality we might as well have hired looters and pirates, traitors and scam artists, to govern us as you can see by the depressed value of our nation in terms of dollars.

There is a possibility that shares in AMERICA 2.0, Inc. will go much higher than this in value due to an increase in the value of all these assets, a gradual reduction in our national liabilities and worker productivity. Then, there is the question of a Price to Earnings Multiple. The current value of $2.10 per Share today in America 1.0 is based on NO MULTIPLE in the price of the shares and that seems right to me as I write this given the scope and range of pessimism and stock market deleveraging going on today.

In my opinion, giving the American people stock ownership in their country would incentivize us all to work at double or even triple our current rate of productivity. So, it is highly possible that at some time in the future, however, that Shares in America 2.0, could go skyrocketing in value with a Multiple of even 10 times, that would make for a Share Value of $21.00 Per Share and with an increase in earnings and so forth, the value could go up in terms of supply and demand for these shares all over the world from people looking for a safe place to put their money and this could drive our shares in future to $200 to $300 Per Share or possibly even MUCH MORE.

Always the optimist, I'm sure that in my lifetime, I could see such a value returning to our shares as we begin to reinvent the American way of life and become far less dependent on foreign oil, boost the technical aspects of our economy, etc. BUT, as our value stands today, $1.75 IS SIMPLY UNACCEPTABLE and spells disaster for us all if the value of our shares in the economy were to fall any lower!

We can and we MUST do something about this. Are we going to wait until the value of America goes down to ZERO? What then? Will we be able to do anything about our economy at that point? This SAD FACT represents an AVERAGE total value of our holdings in America PER WORKER at: 10,000 shares X $1.75 = $17,500 This may sound like a large number for the average American to have in assets in their country.

We could do much better if we ran this country like a business. Yet, it's worse than this. We must now take the Total National Debt and calculate that value per person because we ALL OWE THIS MONEY to the rest of the world and to each other. That amounts to approximately $100,000 for every man woman and child in America today. Let's look at this dismal figure PER FAMILY to make more sense of it. Per Family, the National Debt Amount is approximately $200,000. Now, take the Net Asset Value of all our Shares in

America at present time Per Household = $35,000 That means that the value of our SHARES in AMERICA at PRESENT after taking account of our National Debt is approximately: $153.000 or Negative One Hundred and Fifty-Three Thousand Dollars Per Family. We're all in the RED folks.

Sorry to be the bearer of this news. Now, since our government on a Profit and Loss basis is currently losing about 500 Billion Dollars Per year, and next year, due to the errant Bush Wars, Bank Bail Outs and so-called Obama Rescue Plans, plus all the economic stimulus plans on the books, our government will be losing around TWO TRILLION DOLLARS PER YEAR, starting next year.

That means that the VALUE of our SHARES is depreciating at a rate of about 20% Per Year and at this current rate of real Dollar LOSS of our Government (AKA the Federal Budget Deficit), we will have a NET SHARE VALUE in five years of ZERO. That's not really good for what used to be the richest nation on Earth. Now, this dismal accounting is based on the CASE that we are all ISSUED STOCK TODAY in America TODAY and we have to calculate a starting point in the number of shares.

We could receive less shares or more shares, but the value would equal the same per share. We obviously have a great deal of work to do to bring the value of our shares in America up to a decent and respectable account value. After looking at the problem from this very pragmatic way and assessing the TRUE VALUE of SHARES in AMERICA at the present time, the way I see things shaping up with the share distribution formula that we will announce later, is that we should all accumulate around 100,000 shares by the time we retire at age 60.

Yes, that's right, we should all aim to retire a little early. Age 66, the current Social Security Retirement age is forced on us due to the horrible state of the Social Security System with more and more people retiring and fewer and fewer people actually working and paying taxes into the system to support the retirees. As discussed earlier, we should all automatically receive stock in America when we're born as a kind of down payment, let's say 100 Shares.

Then, when we get our first full time salaried position, we should receive another 100 Shares. When we stay with our company, that loyalty and hard work and devotion to our employer should earn us another let's say 500 Shares for each YEAR with the company. And, it should start over when we change employers. When we achieve something that the company sees as real value for the other employees, we should be awarded with BONUS shares, such as 1,000 Shares for inventing something that receives a patent and is marketable. Or receive another 1,000 Shares in America for writing a hit song, producing a best selling book, making a blockbuster movie, creating a new product or service, or even for raising a child to the age of 18, being a homemaker, etc.

We will be taking suggestions on the many ways that we all agree should result in Bonused Shares to workers. The point being reached that by the time we retire, we should all be able to accumulate enough Shares in America to support us for the rest of our lives through good health or bad. That means to me that we should have reached by Retirement Age an average of approximately 100,000 Shares, but they should be worth at least $10 Per Share or a net value of ONE MILLION DOLLARS. That's right, every American should be able to reach retirement with assets of at least ONE MILLION DOLLARS. Think about it for a minute. Counting all the health costs as high as they are, the cost of housing, food, energy etc. and the fact that a retired person should NOT have to work hard any more at this stage in life, ONE MIILION DOLLARS is just barely sufficient to fill the needs.

However, as we have seen, the bad news today that if we had to retire today even with 100,000 Shares in America, we would owe more than we are worth. Even assuming we have all earned 100,000 shares at today's share value, we would be able to retire with around $210,000 but we all owe $190,000, almost a wash. Isn't it interesting that this is a fairly accurate look at our average situations.

The average Retirement Account today is well under $210,000 and this means that our retirement is actually based on the Net Asset Value of our nation as a whole. We were never told this is how they calculate our personal finances, but this is what it comes down to. It's always about the numbers. Not a very good start to our retirement. And, the money would have to come from somewhere, probably from the value of our shares.

So, how are we going to get a Net Share Value of $10 Per Share or more? We would have to work very hard to build the Total Asset Value of all our corporations and get these corporations out of debt as well as our individual personal account? How can we do all of that when our OWN GOVERNMENT IS WORKING AGAINST US, putting us into debt more and more every day?

The answer is quite simple, we must take the reigns of government in the same way the shareholders today can control the direction of their company. We must have the right to get rid of bad managers in a timely fashion, that is PRIOR to when they RUIN US ALL, as George W. AMBUSH was able to accomplish. There was no way to fire that man outside of the Impeachment Process and the Congress was in his control at the time, so we were all hostages to his sick and heinous ideas.

W must also control things by keeping the government on a very tightly controlled budget process, and the only way to figure out a fair and equitable budget for our government is to incorporate it and put the government on a strict business accounting footing where they have to report to us quarterly and give us progress statements and more importantly have people in the government posts who understand sound Business Principles and can apply them to every department. And, this can only happen if the United States Government is Incorporated where the watchdog procedures, used successfully for the most part for hundreds of years would be employed.

As long as we give them the status of PUBLIC SECTOR, they all know that there is no real accounting and they can use VOODOO ECONOMICS, as mentioned by President George H.W. Bush as relating to the policies of Ronald Reagan. He was actually correct in this assessment of Republican Economic Policy, but unfortunately, he was never taken seriously and he never repeated this phrase when he himself was President and used VOODOO ECONOMICS to put this country even deeper in debt than Reagan.

This is the way Government Officials prefer to do business currently. They never tell us the truth. They always give us the platitudes that they think we want to hear, in order to get elected and to stay in office, and then when they retire, we learn the truth. There is no reporting agency that can shed light on what they do because they are all owned by the government and they bribe our elected officials to do their bidding. So, when it comes time for a little objectivity and clear analysis as you have here in this book, the American People get very little in return for their patience and forbearance.

The truth is that we have been living on a 'Guns and Butter' Economy for the last century, ever since World War II. During World War Two, we fought a global war against two of the strongest military powers in history, Hitler's Germany and Hirohito's Japan. Under a democratic administration, the American people were asked to make sacrifices. Families earned very little money, paid very high taxes to pay for the war and even the wives and mothers went to work in factories to build the bombs and the airplanes that eventually won the war. When we won the war, we were not in any great amount of debt.

War bonds were paid off within ten years and we had basically a clean slate and from there, we went on to build the strongest economy in the history of the world. Since we have had Republican Administrations, however, spending more and more money for wars in Viet Nam and Iraq WITH NO SACRIFICE from the American People AND an inflated cost of war, BILLIONS PER MONTH, we are now one of the weakest economies in the world.

Nixon put us about 2 trillion dollars in debt. Reagan put us another 2 trillion dollars in debt. And the first disastrous war in Iraq under the elder Bush cost us billions per day only to keep Saddam Hussein in power which put us another trillion dollars in debt and this set us up for the worst President in history the son of Bush, who with the complicity of Congress who DOUBLED the NATIONAL DEBT left by his father to its present TEN TRILLION DOLLAR LEVEL and GROWING at around ONE TRILLION PER YEAR NOW. (Update: The Obama Administration increased it to 16 Trillion at the time of this writing.)

In fact, the only respite from this downward spiral of the American Economy was the eight years of President Bill Clinton who erased about a Trillion of the First Bush Debt, left office with a 500 Billion Dollar Surplus, which the younger Bush squandered away completely in his first THREE MONTHS in office. As I have said before, this level of incompetence and malfeasance in office could not possibly be an accident.

For anyone who feels that the Government cannot make a profit has only to recall the Clinton administration. For all his flaws and greed, at least he proved that the government could in fact make a profit. Sadly, instead of paying his 5 Billion Dollar surplus back to the taxpayers in one gigantic refund check, he allowed his successor,

George W. Bush to squander it all within the first few months of his administration, proving that though the Government can, by some freakish miracle, make a profit, we must never rely on them to do so and when given a profit, will promptly throw it all away as fast as they can. Why do they have this attitude about losing our money so rapidly? Because there is no one to stop them. Net yet.

The historic record of our country's steady economic decline under Republican Presidents is ample evidence that it is no accident. It has to be regarded as a strategy of some sort, a plot, a conspiracy, a scheme of some kind because the facts are simply too glaringly obvious. Therefore, in order to reverse this secret policy of the Republican Party, we must refuse them any power in this country from this point forward and we must work very hard with whatever parties are left to work with us, to cooperate with the People to bring up the value of our shares in America.

In order to make all of this completely clear and manifest, we must begin America 2.0, Inc and take stock in the new upgraded version, the business model of our country and put our leaders on notice that they are our employees and they work for us and that we all demand a profit, not a loss every year from the operations of that government, a profit that will inure to the benefit of the people, the shareholders who demand a fair and equitable return on the value of their work and investments of their life times.

HOW TO MAKE GOVERNMENT SCORE PROFITS more than LOSSES.

Currently - the only way that any government has to make profits is to TAX and CHARGE FEES in excess of their spending. For example, in your city, there is a fee charged to homeowners and Apartment building owners to pay for the pick up of garbage and recycling. This agency of the local government is profitable or at least at a break-even. The city collects as much money from the users that can pay for the refuse truck drivers and the trucks to come around to your home every week and take away the garbage and deliver it to the local land fill. Another excellent example of this problem is the Defense Department. America currently spends almost one trillion dollars every year defending the entire free world. Countries like Singapore, the Philippines, Japan have the distinct advantage of being protected from invasion by the US NAVY – FOR FREE.

Most of Europe is defended by the United States Air Force, Navy and the Marines.

Why in the world don't we charge them for this essential service? We don't only because our government is setup as a LOSING PROPOSITION. They more money they lose, the better – or so the thinking goes. Having a strong Defense is something that we must always maintain since we have learned over history that if you are not strong in this world, you will be exploited by others who are strong. But, the Defense Department needs to spend BILLIONS on highly technical airplanes, submarines, aircraft carriers, missiles, bombs etc. and since you cannot use any of these things, except in times of great threat or emergencies, this department of our corporation cannot make a profit.

But, that means that we have to have many other departments that can score profits to pay for our defense. For example, we only have a tax on gasoline of 11 cents federal. This piddling amount is only about 2% of the total cost of a gallon of gasoline. We need to discourage use of gasoline since we have learned that this product produces cancer and global warming as well as just generally polluting our country and our planet. Therefore a consumption tax of 10% or more would be called for.

Since our elected leaders take bribes from the Oil and Car producing corporations, something that will be completely eliminated in America 2.0, Inc. politicians have been reluctant to do the right thing by us and increase this tax, thus ENCOURAGING the use of this toxic product instead of DISCOURAGING it in favor or cleaner alternative fuels. It's only in the last few months, after the general outrage over the quickly rising cost of gasoline at the pumps that some effort has been made to debate this issue. Still nothing has actually been done.

If we taxed this toxic substance appropriately, the Government would have several BILLION MORE dollars per year to help balance the budget and we would all be more encouraged to drive less, conserve energy more and use alternative means of transportation such as bicycles, buses, car pools, trains, etc. which would also have the beneficial effect of reducing traffic, thus wear and tear on our roads and other infrastructure.

So, the general principle of good business in government should be to TAX and HEAVILY FINE those areas of our civilization that is detrimental our health, peace and prosperity. For another example, we should have been heavily taxing our Gas Guzzling cars and Trucks and take the money earned in the last 20 years to invest in the technology of Electric Cars and Trucks powered by clean electricity generated from Solar and Wind power.

But, instead, largely because of the BRIBES that our leaders have taken from the OIL companies and CAR manufacturing and repair Industries, we have done no such thing. Thus the trouble we're in right now, where we send some 700 BILLION DOLLARS PER YEAR to the OPEC nations. This is money that could have been spent on creating Public Transit, cleaner cars, more roads, better hospitals, schools, etc.

In general we want to work for a world where our Defense Spending can be reduced also because we are a country that is less threatening to other countries, our economy is more on an even keel, requiring less sacrifice from foreign countries and that way, we can save money in departments that have no way of making a profit.

We should be helping our neighbors to improve their economies also so that we are not losing jobs to their more desperate work force. We should have had a STRONG TARIFF policy on all imported goods to protect the American workers. Our competitors like China and Japan have very HIGH TARIFFS against American goods, so we end up TAKING all the products they can produce in almost slave labor nations and we get to send them very little of our goods produced in America because of their tariffs.

Is this FAIR and EQUITABLE or even moral? Of course not, and the reason we have UNFAIR and IMMORAL government regulations and laws is always due to the BRIBES that our government leaders take EVEN FROM FOREIGN LOBBYISTS. This to me is TREASON, nothing short and should be punished as one would punish a traitor.

In America 2.0, Inc. we will brook no treason and every law that has a vital and significant impact on our general financial health would have to be approved or VETOED by the VOTERS themselves. More on this in the next chapter – National Ballot Measures.

CHAPTER SEVEN - National Ballot Measures

We all know that Google is very much interested in modernizing this country's infra-structure. They're experimenting with cars that drive themselves and are connected to the Internet at all times. They developed Google Glass so that we can have the Internet right at our birds-eye-view at all times. They allow us to have the Internet on our TV sets, they allow us to download music on Google Play. They are building a higher speed Internet using Fiber-Optics. And, they have that mysterious top-secret barge in San Francisco bay that has antennae protruding from every surface. My guess is this is for blocking the NSA Spying on our computers and smart phones. The reason this equipment is on a barge is because when ready, they will float it out into International waters where the US Government has no jurisdiction.

So, now that we know how serious they are about the infra-structure of this country and the Internet and where both of these things intersect is in the Political Infra-structure and therefore, Google Super-Vote and and will be developed for its highest and best use, but only if enough of our average citizens get on board and start demanding that same thing. Google, like anyone else is surely not going to do anything that isn't popular.

And, the place where we make this a popular idea is at my website first and then on every other web site that you, the reader may influence.

America2inc.com

Google Super-Vote then, will evolve, with your help into actual National Ballot Measures, places on the Federal Election ballot where we get to publish our best ideas and then allow the voters to PASS or REJECT these ideas. Below, you will find several examples of how we will use Google SuperVote as National Ballot Measures.

National Ballot Measures must also be the keystone to our NEW Corporate Foundation of Government. As we have discussed earlier, one of the keystones to America 2.0, Inc, is finally a REAL DEMOCRACY in AMERICA and a model of Democracy for the rest of the world. Only way we are going to get Real Democracy and a Real New Country is to give the people more power to control our destiny. The biggest hurdle that we face is that Congress, due to their own incompetence, and being bribed every day by the lobbyists - will NEVER DO the RIGHT THING in a vast majority of cases. The Republic is dead.

Any Republic will die every time that the representatives will not pass laws that generally support the middle class because they take bribes, they call them campaign contributions, from Corporations who want to either block laws that support the general public or pass laws that give them the laws the way they want them to impact their bottom line profits.

In fact, they have already killed the Republic and the proof is heard on the radio, published in newspapers or seen on TV every day. You only have to open your eyes to see the death throes of this once-great nation. They argue and debate an issue for decades before actually getting them on the floor of Congress for a vote. By then, the problem has already done it's worst. Just like a virus, the bad things in this world go around and infect us one by one until we're either dead or we've somehow survived. By the time our present form of government gets around to a real cure, those who were infected, have passed away or have survived, but they are also reduced in their health by the virus. Then, Congress may come along 25 to 30 years later - too late to do any good - with a vaccine. The vaccine is completely ineffective because the problem has evolved and now has a completely different DNA structure and will not be effected by this cure. And, so on and on this vicious cycle goes. All of it caused by one major problem that we must solve first - money in politics.

The only reason, the entire Congress is not thrown out of office for BRIBERY is that THEY are the ones who get to DEFINE BRIBERY under the LAW. They specifically have drafted laws to MAKE IT LEGAL to take BRIBES by this method of bribery. But, calling this antidemocratic and destructive process, 'CAMPAIGN CONTRIBUTIONS' is defying all logic and morality. AND the PROOF IS that THEY NEVER GIVE BACK any portion of their CAMPAIGN CONTRIBUTIONS that were not used for CAMPAIGNING.

The money sits there for years, gather interest, until their campaigns are over and then magically, it disappears. Not a single contributor even asks to get their remaining money back because that would be against the rules and they would be discriminated against by the next campaigner OR maybe they just don't think about money that has been spent.

If you don't believe that our democracy has been stolen by this method of BRIBERY, just ask yourself, "When did the Congress last pass a law that did anything for me?" You'll quickly realize that all the recent laws, such as the New Bankruptcy laws were passed FOR THE BANKS, and made it tougher for a consumer to declare bankruptcy and get even with the crooked banks that charge up to 50% Interest on the unsuspecting and naive borrowers. The drug laws were passed to support the DRUG COMPANIES, not the people who are sick and need the drugs. So, tens of thousands of our American families are forced to go bankrupt, under very STRICT BANKING LAWS, passed by the BANKS to PROTECT BANKS, after we are FORCED TO SPEND OURSELVES INTO BANKRUPTCY by the laws that were passed to protect the Health and Drug Industries. Is that Democracy? I don't think so.

Therefore, there are several REAL CHANGES we must make to our system of government in order to RECOVER OUR DEMOCRACY, strengthen it, and make it INSURMOUNTABLE and IMPREGNABLE for all future generations to come.

The introduction of National Ballot Measures is the keystone to accomplishing this because with a DIRECT WAY of counting the ELECTORS, US, AS THE KEY PEOPLE REPRESENTED IN THE LAWS of this nation. ONE OF THE FIRST NATIONAL BALLOT MEASURES WE MUST TAKE IS TO ABOLISH LOBBYING by MAKING IT A FELONY to LOBBY anyone in Congress.

Any person or organization who pays any money or gives any benefits to any elected Official or Appointee in the United States Government should be punished by DEATH, or at least enough money in FINES and JAIL TERMS to make it highly UNLIKELY that anyone would want to take the chance. By PLACING SOLUTIONS to OUR MAJOR NATIONAL PROBLEMS ON THE BALLOT and then ALLOWING the People to DEBATE them and then VOTE ON THEM DIRECTS, we OUTWIT, OUTSMART and OUTLAST (Just like in the TV Show SURVIVOR) the LOBBYISTS and all other special interests who strive to CONSTANTLY INFLUENCE our GOVERNMENT and subvert the will of the MAJORITY of voters, the SHAREHOLDERS, the REAL OWNERS of this country.

In 2009, Lobbyists spent over THREE BILLION DOLLARS in bribes to Congress. This was a RECORD year for this kind of investment in government. Will Rogers once said, "We have the best Congress money can buy." And he would be even more right today. When it's legal for business interests to BRIBE the men and women who were elected to represent their constituents, ordinary people, it's time for a real change.

The Divine Right of Kings discussed earlier is very safe and secure in the world once again and the founding fathers of this great nation are turning over in their graves at what they are witnessing. We CAN and we MUST find new ways of doing the business of government to bring the principles of good government back into alignment with the real reason for having a government, to improve and protect the lives of the greatest majority of citizens who's lives are impacted on any given issue.

As we write this book, President Obama is struggling mightily, paying a great deal of attention to ONE PROBLEM, the Health Insurance Reform package that Congress created for him. The President of the United States, while we have enemies around every corner is having to spell out for members of his own party and even more for members of the Republican Party that Health Care is in crisis and must be reformed, which we all know to be true. How to do that is the question of the day.

Just as an aside: What's even more incredibly wasteful and hideous about the first four years of the Obama Administration is that the US Supreme Court is probably going to rule Obama Care, at least the most important part of it, the mandate, the requirement that everyone must purchase health insurance in this country to be UNCONSTITUTIONAL. Now, how funny is that? We voted these people into office and the only real accomplishment is to produce something that they had to have known would be THROWN OUT. This is your government in action, folks. An entire four years of the Obama administration, at least on this issue, has been totally squandered. The War in Afghanistan ranks right up there with Obamacare, however as being totally useless and wasteful to the tune of TRILLIONS of our dollars and countless lives lost.

NOW, let's look at this question in light of this author's concept of converting everything in Government to making a profit. First of all, it would be very difficult to make a profit in the area of Health Care UNDER the PRESENT THEOLOGY of the NEED TO LOSE MONEY. For example, Medicare is known to spend about 100 Billion Dollars per year in FRAUDULENT PAYMENTS. Most of the other Federal Agencies have similar accounting irregularities. Why can this go one? Because A. No one is in charge and B. Because they can. They're part of a non-profit, so who cares? And C. It's not their money, so why worry.

IF we start from the premise that the government has to MAKE A PROFIT, however, things get much rosier. The only bill that the President or Congress should really be proposing, if they sincerely want to solve this Health Care Crisis is to make it EASIER and CHEAPER for INSURANCE COMPANIES TO FORM and ENTER the exchange, the common pool of insurance carriers that anyone can access across state lines.

It's the most basic foundation of economics that when you have more competition in any given market, prices for that product are forced to go down. So, it would be for the Health Insurance Industry if there were hundreds of Insurance Companies for the consumer to choose from instead of the dozen or so in existence today. There are so few insurance companies around today because the Insurance Companies bought and paid for our United States Congressmen and Senators.

The House of Representatives just now, while writing this book passed a law that TAKES AWAY the ANTI-TRUST exemption enjoyed by Insurance Companies for decades and the main reason that there is no real price competition in this industry. The HOUSE passed this bill. It will be a miracle if the Senate passes it, the only way it can become law, because a few Senators in the right COMMITTEES in the Senate can block any legislation like this and they will block it because they are taking bribes from the Insurance Industry who are HELL_BENT on keep control over the American people.

It will never pass the Senate, I guarantee you that because now the Insurance companies have set their last stand by bribing the Committee Chairman who actually has the power to put things on the floor of the Senate for a vote. If that one man doesn't want that bill to see the light of day and be voted on in Congress all he does is SIT ON IT. And one check if it's large enough will cause that one man to sit on this bill. It will never become LAW - watch and see.

How can that be true, you are asking yourself? It's true - because they can. We The People have no voice to stand up and DENY them this much power. One Vote on Google Super Vote as a Ballot Measure would STOP THIS TRAVESTY of democracy and justice immediately and at no cost to the American people. If we had Google Super-Vote in place today, this is the first thing I would use it for. AND, the solution is so simple.

ON THE BALLOT you would see the following:

AS OF (A DATE 90 Days from the Election) Anyone in Congress shall have the ability to put a bill before Congress and all members of Congress must vote on it.

DONE:

Would YOU VOTE FOR THAT? Because it eliminates the power of the ONE-MAN in Senate or House and distributes equal power through the entire Congress.

BUT a much BETTER BALLOT MEASURE would be to simply make it a FELONY to give any politicians money or anything of value under a heavy penalty of ten years in prison and one million dollars in fines.

That would help too. But, BOTH of these Ballot Measures working together would finally get our country back, would they not?

At least it's a start in the right direction. Would you vote for both of these Google SuperVote National Ballot Measures? If you love your country and desire to see it advance and prosper, I think you would.

Just ask yourself - How just two or three individuals in Congress have gained the power to BLOCK legislation in a DEMOCRACY is totally beyond any common sense or acceptable approach by any measure? Yet this is the system under which we suffer.

So, the Health Care Crisis gives us a good microscope through which we can investigate how our nation must make fundamental changes and where. If we allow these Lobbyists to continue to influence our lawmaking, then there is never going to come a day in which our government can make a profit and MUCH WORSE the problems that we face as a civilization can never really be solved. Under our current system, the major problems of the country are obfuscated and fogged up by so much rhetoric that everyone scratches their heads and goes about their business and they want us to remain apathetic because it's under this fog of war that they can control us in the back rooms, the deal making rooms on K-Street where the 50,000 Lobbyists hone their skills.

A simple bill making it easier for anyone to form an insurance company and then enter the Insurance Coverage Pool for anyone in the country to call and get a quote, would INSTANTLY SOLVE our HEALTH CARE CRISIS at least at this level, the Insurance Level.

But, the basic underlying problem as to why our Health Insurance costs so much has to be because the Health Care itself is too expensive. If we had companion legislation that also made room for PREVENTIVE MEDICINE then the cost of our Health Care would go to about HALF of where it is now and that would also translate into cheaper Health Care Insurance, wouldn't it?

BUT, we don't get the proper attention paid to PREVENTIVE medicine in this country because again the Hospital and Doctor lobbyists as well as the Pharmaceutical companies DON'T REALLY WANT US TO BE HEALTHY. This would cause them too much money if we were all healthy, so they spend BILLIONS in LOBBYING to influence our government to keep them in business. IF WE TOOK a MORE HOLISTIC APPROACH to preventing DISEASES in the first place, we would not be having this national debate currently about how to REFORM HEALTH CARE.

REFORM OUR UNHEALTHY LIFESTYLES first, and then Health Care will become far more reasonable. CASE IN POINT, our cars and factories pour so much toxic waste into the atmosphere, the ground, the water, the oceans that we are poisoning our systems from the day we are born until the day we are finally forced into a hospital to cure our asthma, our cancer, etc. And, there is no cure to these types of problems because we are POISONING our systems every day in the way we get ourselves around the planet.

If the OIL INDUSTRY no longer had this massive influence over us, the toxins from this industry and all the related ones like the PLASTICS INDUSTRY and even DRUG INDUSTRIES would be reduced to zero. Thus our individual health would improve and the need for Health Care services greatly reduced. Supply and demand takes over and the cost of these things would have to go down dramatically. Instead of this holistic approach to Government and Health because they are intertwined in so many ways, we instead are going into the doctor's offices, hospitals and clinics at ever increasing rates and we have our own environmental health to blame.

IF Government were TRULY OF, BY and FOR the PEOPLE, instead of the INDUSTRY LOBBYISTS who ply them with money every day, we would have a more HOLISTIC approach to Government, Health and everything else and we would lead much happier lives. We can and must have more COMMON SENSE LAWS in this country, but ONLY UNTIL AND UNLESS we change our basic system allowing for Government to make PROFITS and for the SHAREHOLDERS TO VOTE in their best interests, thus killing forever the FULL NELSON WRESTING HOLD that INDUSTRY LOBBYISTS have over us.

Our Congress cannot think in terms of anything that even smacks of common sense because of all the money that they have to accept from the lobbyists who are yelling and screaming at them louder than any average American Citizen can because they are YELLING and HOLDING MILLIONS of DOLLARS in their hands. This gets their attention. If you've ever tried calling or talking to or even writing a letter to your Congressman or woman, you know how fast they spit out the response letters telling you how wonderful you are and what a great thing it is in our democracy that you can write a letter or make a phone call and someone is listening.

OH YEAH, that's what their letters say, and we PAY MILLIONS of dollars every year, it's in their budgets, to print and mail these meaningless letters. But, at the end of the day, they go to a conference hosted by a major Oil Company or a Major Insurance company. They're wined and dined and fly around in a fancy corporate jet to any luxury resort you care to name.

And, then, how do they vote on this problem? In ways that continue to maintain the MONOPOLY that the Insurance Companies, the Oil Companies, the Banks, etc. have over us. This is SO DISGUSTING and the proof is for you to ask your Congressman or Senator why they don't just SIMPLIFY the INSURANCE COMPANY RULES so that many HUNDREDS MORE could be created and enter into the pool and see what he says.

This is a PRIME example of the free enterprise system that they often tout they are trying to protect, but when it comes to any real free enterprise, they only mean to have it defended for their CONTRIBUTORS and no others. THIS FAVORITISM and FELONIOUS LOBBYING has to end or we are doomed. Instead of a good COMMON SENSE APPROACH to Health Care Reform, they are struggling today to pass a 2,400 Page Bill that will cost us almost ONE TRILLION DOLLARS to put into effect.

We cannot afford the TRILLIONS already wasted, why throw good money after bad? I must add, that the REAL UNDERLYING problem to our Health Care Crisis is the COST of the HEALTH CARE in the first place. It costs hundreds of dollars to visit the doctor, thousands to visit the hospital and God Forbid, you contract a life threatening disease, unless you have very costly health insurance, this disease will take all your assets away from you. So much so that forty five thousand people every year in this country decide to let themselves die, rather than get the treatment they need simply because they cannot afford the treatment. FORTY FIVE THOUSAND PEOPLE every year, die because they cannot afford the health care that would have saved their lives.

This is 50 times worse than the damage caused by 9/11 and it happens every year. Congress should be ashamed that they allow us to die every year in such great numbers. Not only should they be ashamed, they should be incarcerated as conspirators.

So – WHAT is the SOLUTION to nearly all our government ills?

It's time to ALLOW THE WILL Of the MAJORITY STAKE HOLDERS to make the RULES. In a Democracy, it is always the WILL OF THE MAJORITY OF VOTERS, the MAJORITY OF CITIZENS, that MAKE the DECISIONS, not the WILL of the FEW, the Connected, the Cronies, the CROOKS.

This is what we have to suffer today, but this is NOT DEMOCRACY and this form of Government CORRUPTS DEMOCRACY and gives it such a bad name that many people SHUN DEMOCRACY, thinking this is IT.

IT IS NOT. What we have now is RIDICULOUS. It's a joke. It's an INSULT to all thinking Americans and it must be put to rest. NATIONAL BALLOT MEASURES, especially as the Keystone of America 2.0, Inc. can never only WORK to SERVE and SAVE the Majority, always the best way to make a DECISION or any series of decisions in any situation.

WHAT FOLLOWS are EXAMPLES ONLY of NATIONAL BALLOT MEASURES. Don't rush to the polls to vote on these issues. We do NOT yet have the right to vote on National Initiatives like these. We do have the right to vote on State Initiatives in 22 of the states, but NOT ON THE FEDERAL BALLOT to either pass or veto any Federal Laws. WHY NOT?

UPDATE: IF a NATIONAL BALLOT MEASURE were held during this NOVEMBER'S GENERAL PRESIDENTIAL ELECTION, the most obvious choice would be the FOLLOWING. How much would you like to see this on the BALLOT?

Measure A. "We the People do hereby vote to ABOLISH the ELECTORAL COLLEGE method of deciding Presidential Elections. From this point forward, all elections for President of the United States shall be decided by a majority of the overall POPULAR VOTE from all states."

This is a no-brainer folks, especially when we remember that George W. Bush, the worst President in our History as a nation was forced on the total American Population and the population of the world by a few religious screwballs in a few of the Bible Belt Red States and their Electoral College members, whoever the hell they are.

If the POPULAR VOTE was the "DECIDER", the majority of American Voters actually VOTING in the ELECTION, we would have had Al Gore as President and I doubt seriously that he would have invaded the wrong country. He would not have spent us into bankruptcy and he would have cleaned up both Washington and the Environment.

We might also be driving ELECTRIC CARS powered by solar panels on all our roofs and the Health and prosperity of the Middle

Class American would be BETTER BY FIVE OR TEN FOLD. OUR FAMILY INCOMES would be at least $7,500 per year greater on average, just as it happened in the CLINTON years. There would have been no Mortgage Meltdown, the Stock Market would NOT have crashed and the price of gasoline would be 99 cents again, OR LESS, because it would have to compete with FREE SOLAR and WIND GENERATED ELECTRICITY to power our cars.

The Electoral College can be manipulated by a few clever CROOKS that the parties can use in their campaigns to steal elections. ONE MAN, ONE VOTE is the only honest way to elect a President, just as we elect everyone else. Why should the MOST POWERFUL OFFICE in the world be held to a different corruptible standard? This was a method devised over two centuries AGO, when there were no better ways of collecting votes other than by horse and buggy. Times have changed, so have the issues.

Measure B. "We the People do hereby vote to REJECT the Bail out the banks and Wall Street under the Bush Administration's proposals of paying $700 Billion of Tax Payer dollars and buying worthless assets. Instead we favor a Let them Fail approach. It is NOT in the best interests of the American People or Democracy in General to allow thieves to steal from us and then reward thieves with a bail out that essentially allows them so start all over." HOW WOULD YOU VOTE ON THIS ISSUE?

And - WHY IS THIS NOT ON THE BALLOT? WHY WAS IT DONE UNDER George W. AMBUSH? These are questions that every American Citizen should be asking themselves today.

The only reason we don't vote directly on the issues in a Real Democracy is simply because no one has demanded this right as of today.

BUT - this right is guaranteed to us under Article Nine of the Constitution which reads as follows:

"The enumeration in the Constitution, of certain rights, shall not be construed to deny or disparage others retained by the people."

This ONE SENTENCE in our Constitution is quite clear and means exactly what it says. I interpret it as follows. Can you claim any other interpretation?

"We the Founding Fathers of this great country can't think of everything and in fact, we left out lots of stuff that you'll need in the future because, none of us having crystal balls, we can't see into the future, but we suspect that your government will become highly corrupted over the years and so you will require further rights to control the evil that is done to you and to ensure that it never happens again - or all is lost."

Now, this is almost like Channeling Ben Franklin, Tom Jefferson, good friends of mine, because these thoughts are taken directly from some of their famous quotes. Ben Franklin said, when leaving the Constitutional Convention of 1789 that created this great document when asked by a lady what kind of government they had given us, he said, "A Republic madam, if you can keep it." Of course, we didn't keep it. As I've mentioned earlier, nothing in our government today smacks like a Republic. It's now a tyrannical dictatorship of a few very wealthy elite.

And Thomas Jefferson said, "You'll need to have a bloody Revolution every 20 years or so, if you want to remain free." So, the founding fathers knew that "Power corrupts and absolute Power Corrupts, absolutely." And, they predicted that things would not remain as they would like in any future generations. They were correct.

AND, therefore, in accordance with the 9th Amendment, we must now make another one that gives us the power to end this mad dash to oblivion that we are on. We must amend the US Constitution so that We The People have the power to control these corrupt forces and help our government solve our problems in a manner that is beneficial to all, not to just a select few.

The Twenty Eighth Amendment to the United States Constitution: N.B.M.A.

The National Ballot Measure Amendment

"Section 1. The right of citizens of the United States to vote on issues they deem the most urgent and of National importance through the process of a National Initiative ballot measure which must pass by a two-thirds majority of voters, and qualified for the National Ballot by the signatures of two percent of the registered voters in any twenty-five of the states, or through a National Referendum placed on the ballot by a vote of three fourths of Congress shall not be denied or abridged by the United States or by any state.

Section 2. The Congress shall have power to enforce this article by appropriate legislation."

Pretty Simple Amendment and you may be asking yourself why is this power not already granted to the People of the United States when thirty-two states use this same process to settle issues that effect their individual states?

If the process of Initiatives and Referenda are useful in thirty-two states, why would it not be useful on the Federal Level? And more importantly, you must ask yourselves why the greatest level of leadership in this land has not recommended it to you before now? The answer to that question is simple.

They want to keep the power over your fate where it rests now, in their hands and in their hands solely. If it were not, bribery would be a thing of the past, their multi-million dollar pensions might be in jeopardy if we the people didn't think we needed them so much. And why not give the American people this true measure of democracy now?

We can much more easily and quickly VOTE ON THE ISSUES DIRECTLY. Don't listen to their lies about SECURITY. The results of an Internet Election can be LOCKED DOWN beyond any system they now have for us to use. In the last Presidential Election millions of votes are still in doubt because the voting machines may have been compromised by a company that donated millions of dollars to the REPUBLICAN PARTY.

THE INTERNET is too big and too redundant to be overpowered by any single group. Integrity and Security is coded into the basic design of the Internet. It was created to be used in case of WORLD WAR THREE and is a network of computers so vast that even if the ENEMY destroyed the vast majority of this country, the INTERNET IS DESIGNED TO KEEP FUNCTIONING. It is the MOST SECURE of any invention in the history of the world. It can be improved certainly and it will be by the time this highest and best form of Democracy becomes the law of the land.

If the founding fathers were creating the national system of democracy, today, with the technology at hand, they would most assuredly put all of the power of freedom to use and not just the puny engine of democracy that you still have now. They could not do so in their day because they had no knowledge that such a system of telecommunications and transportation would ever exist. In their day, there weren't even any paved roads anywhere, just the mud streets that horses could travel. All of the nations goods were transported by horseback and carriage and all of the nation's best ideas were transported by horses too. And so, in this way, democracy was born. Today, it comes of age.

By working for the Twenty-Eighth Amendment, the National Initiative and Referendum Amendment, you will be doing God's work because this is true Freedom as I have said. I have given you more and more freedom over the generations and you have used it wisely, by and large. Freedom cannot be taken lightly, however, and the responsibilities are huge. You must become better educated on the issues and on the history and the ecology of our planet. You must be willing to spend a portion of your day discussing these most important issues confidently and patiently, until you know in your hearts that you have all the information to make the best decisions. And you must not rest until this is done. You must tell everyone you know. You must make copies of my words and let all the others read them and you must debate them first.

When we are all convinced that these suggestions are the right direction to take, you must take action by forcing this amendment on your government for they will not pas it for you easily. They will resist the will for more democracy even though they are sworn to serve you, the majority of people, they don't believe that giving you the power to make decisions is in your best interest, but this is colored by their own desire for their own best interests. You must not let them prevail.

The power of this great nation is vested in the power of the people after all. At the end of the day, you have your greatest minds to rely on who have given you the power to change your government at any time as you please. 'Abraham Lincoln said that we are "A nation, of the people, by the people and for the people."

The Constitution gives you the right to amend the Constitution at any time as stated under Article Five: 'The Congress, whenever two thirds of both Houses shall deem it necessary, shall propose amendments to this Constitution, or, on the Application of the Legislatures of two thirds of the several States, shall call a Convention for proposing Amendments, which, in either Case, shall be valid to all Intents and Purposes, as Part of this Constitution, when ratified by the Legislatures of three fourths of the several

States, or by Conventions in three fourths thereof, as the one or the other Mode of Ratification may be proposed by the Congress.' So, there's the pathway open to us in a legal and forthright manner.

By working for REAL DEMOCRACY AMENDMENT and the 29th Amendment making this GOVERNMENT a CORPORATION, to the United States Constitution, there shall never be any need for any more because all the rest of what we need to do as a NATION can be decided By the People, From the People and For the People. THE FOLLOWING is just a partial list, a few out of HUNDREDS of things WE CAN DECIDE TO DO for ourselves and our posterity.

National Ballot Measure -Examples:

Example 1: A Federal Law requiring that all full time salaried jobs be paid on the basis of a Four Day Work Week. Or put another way, The Three Day Week-end.

Debate: The American worker is the most productive worker on the planet. They have worked so hard and sacrificed so much over the last two hundred years to become the world's number one greatest economy. This law would reward the people of America for a job well done. They would finally be able to enjoy life a little more, spend quality time with their families, recreate, have real leisure which is the goal of civilization since time began. If left to Congress to pass such a law into being, Big Business, with their army of bribery lawyers would bribe every one they could find in office to defeat such a law, but on the ballot there is nothing they could do.

Why not have such a new reality? There once was a time when the average American was forced to work every day. Then, the unions pushed for a couple days of rest and the week-end was born. The Two-Day weekend is a reality that we've all accepted and not one of us would prefer to go back to working seven days a week, I can assure you of that.

And, just as much could be accomplished in four days that is now accomplished in five for most people. Why not give the rest of the world a model for working and resting and enjoying life that would last as the standard for hundreds of years? It was the unions through much strife and struggle got the country to live on a Five Day Work week. Why should you have to wait for another great movement with all the concurrent stresses on society to achieve this kind of social advancement? Why not let this type of decision be decided by the ordinary people, those who work for a living, instead of those who pretend to work in Washington?

Example #2: A Federal Law requiring that whenever a Freeway is built with Federal Highway Funds that at least one lane must be used for mass transit alternatives such as light rail, busses, or carpool lanes or a better way into the future, a computer guided Electric Vehicle Preferred lanes, in order to reduce the dependence on gasoline powered cars.

Debate: Oddly enough, there is no national law requiring mass transit be built anywhere. This is due to the Congress being bought and paid for by the army of bribery officials from the automotive and oil industry who have their offices right next door to Senate offices in Washington, D.C.

I can't think of any reasonable debate against this one. I'm sure the oil industry or the auto industry will concoct something.

Example #3: A limit of One Billion Dollars allocated to the C.I.A. The actual budget of the Top-Secret intelligence agency is currently a secret, but since they can't keep a secret very well, everyone knows it's about Ten Billion Dollars per year and growing. The money allocated to it is a complete and total waste.

Proof is the fact that they did nothing to stop the twenty amateur terrorists who were able to gain Passports under false names, driver's licenses, and have access to Airports and even Airliner training courses. When the head of the C.I.A., George Tenet, did finally receive information from his subordinates on August 23, just a few weeks, plenty of time to prevent the events of September Eleventh that Terrorists were planning to hijack Airliners and fly them into the World Trade Center, he tossed this information into the garbage.

He wasn't even fired for this greatest government negligence in office and instead was rewarded with a Million Dollar Pension and the nation's highest honor, the Medal of Freedom by the President of the United States George W. AMBUSH. Hmmmm, sounds fishy, doesn't it? Perhaps they were in collusion.

Why spend this kind of money on a useless bureaucracy such as this? Put this fact together with the fact that the first order of President of the United States immediately following September Eleventh was not to go and find the perpetrators but instead was to gather up all the relatives of Osama Bin Laden, the single most responsible party, and fly them under Government Escort out of the United States without even being questioned, and you have the essence of why your government needs to be changed drastically from the ground up. You impeached a President for authorizing a petty burglary into an office of the Watergate Hotel.

Sure we need national security so limit the CIA to enough money that will keep us SECURE, but more money makes us more INSECURE.

For some reason, no one in government after these history changing events suggests even a hearing into why these two events are so suspicious and what they could imply. Instead, they appear to have successfully white washed it all up in commissions and reports by commissions created by the government itself. This is possible only because no one is heard, all dissent is blocked. Free Speech is gone. Freedom of assembly is gone when the police can require any organization to acquire PERMITS to ASSEMBLE peacefully.

Freedom of the Press is gone. What precious Freedom will they take from you next? This lack of interest and probing into the truth of such a serious matter is the greatest danger to your democracy, and not these misguided and murderous suicide bombers from the world's most forsaken places.

By limiting the budget of the C.I.A. to One Billion dollars, you will A. Make this empty and useless bureaucracy do more with less and B. You dilute their power over you until such time as you can replace the culture of this bureaucracy with people you can trust. The massive budget of Ten Billion Dollars ore more is obviously wasted on bureaucratic bumbling and could be spent on much more productive projects. The current Budget of the C.I.A. was blown up out of proportion and made a secret due to the Cold War and the necessity of not allowing the Soviet Union to know what we were doing to thwart their plans.

The Cold War has ended and now you need a more streamlined intelligence force capable of finding the amateur little terrorists who using little more than cell phones and box cutters can bring your nation to its knees. Ten billion dollars per year is overkill to find, locate and neutralize people of this kind, if you rearrange your method of operations in how you gather intelligence and what you do with it once gained.

A good companion Initiative to this one would be to abolish the present Pension Plans of all government workers and replace them with a Pension based on merit. When someone in service to the people accomplishes something, they should receive stock in America 2.0 Inc. Several of these stock distributions throughout their career should entitle them to a pension, and nothing less. No distributions should result in no pension. And remember, all agencies would be required to make a profit, so things would be much much different.

If you accomplish nothing throughout twenty or thirty years of your work, why should a person deserve to be rewarded by the people with a lifetime pension? It bears asking. How can the head of the C.I.A. justify his pension after he personally ignored the warning about an event that resulted in the death of thousands of Americans and crippled the American economy for decades? It would be a different matter if he had taken this information to the Federal Aviation Administration, another office, just a few minutes drive from his own, had a few meetings to help them focus on ways of preventing airplane hijackings and hijackers from getting into the cockpits of planes.

If he had just placed a phone call to the office down the street, his counterpart, the head of the F.B.I. and shared this information with this top cop, perhaps one of the millions of F.B.I. agents might have uncovered enough to prevent this from happening by finding these people and holding them for questioning. This is not asking too much. This is the sworn duty of these men. Anything, even one meeting on the subject with another person or agency capable of preventing such a disaster might have entitled him to his Million-Dollar Retirement. This one man, so important in the overall scheme of things will receive millions of dollars from hard working Americans in his government pension and other benefits for doing absolutely nothing about the greatest crime in history of which he had knowledge beforehand. In doing nothing to prevent this tragedy, not even trying, doesn't he deserve nothing?

But it should be noted that instead of Firing HUNDREDS of Government workers who let this happen to us, they merely established a NEW BUREAUCRACY to oversee the old one that failed, setting us all up for an even BIGGER LEVEL of FAILURE. Thus the Department of Homeland Security was formed with another budget in the BILLIONS and thousands of new bureaucrats to sit in nice comfy offices with nothing to do except make up a completely new set of rules such as requiring us all to take our shoes off at the airports before boarding our planes. Yeah, that was worth it.

This kind of thing cannot continue if Freedom is to remain in this world. Take my word for it. The Billions of Tax Dollars saved could much more effectively be spent on improving the nation's schools, the roads, the hospitals, the transportation systems. Nothing is worse than wasting money on frivolous government bureaucracies that accomplish nothing for their own people.

It's We The People, these agencies are created to serve, not their own selfish interests. This focus on self-interest in government must be met with the ultimate weapon at every challenge, the power of the people to bring common sense back into their own system of governance.

Example #4: A Federal Tax Credit for anyone buying and using an automobile powered by a clean burning fuel, such as hydrogen, natural gas or no fuel at all such as an electric powered or human powered vehicle to get to work every day. Debate: Oddly enough, there is no tax credit for the use of alternative vehicles and there sorely needs to be one to encourage the research and development into this field.

This type of legislation would be easily and quickly passed as a NATIONAL BALLOT MEASURE but as an act of Congress, it takes decades, IF AT ALL, to get something worthwhile like this on the books, due to the influence of the oil companies and the automotive industry who like to keep things the same even at the cost of the health of their own planet.

Example #5: A Federal Law raising the limit of income that is taxed for Social Security taxes up to One Million Dollars annually, thus solving the Social Security Cash Flow problems for all time.

Debate: The President of the United States has told you all with no room for uncertainty that he believes Social Security is in trouble due to the ratio of workers to retirees having dropped over the years and people living longer. This alternative, which is the most obvious and the simplest and least costly of all alternatives to solving this problem was not acceptable to the President as of the time of this writing. There are indications that he may change his mind, however, the Republican Party has made statements that they would never support any such tax raise to solve the problem so easily and quickly.

This Ballot Initiative, most likely placed on the ballot by Americans who are approaching retirement age and are concerned about losing their benefits the soonest, would give the people themselves, those most effected by this issue to decide for themselves if they cared to rescue America's greatest social entitlement plan in this way.

This is perhaps one of the best examples of how Congress can be your worst enemy sometimes. Whenever there is a perceived problem in this nation, instead of honest debate on the issues, they have taken the attitude that it is best to deceive the American people and to confuse them by putting out so much baloney and horse manure to the media that you will all become so tired and worn down by their constant bickering that eventually, you will think they are wise and have your interests at heart.

This is perhaps the greatest trickery ever performed on such a large scale in the history of the world. When a problem like this is brought to your attention, the most important thing for you to do as a nation of patriotic Americans is to think about the most logical, the fairest to everyone involved and the easiest solution, not a solution that makes matters worse as they want to do in Congress. When Congress brings forth their proposed solutions and they sound as if they are coming from the army of bribery officers that they have at their beck and call at all times, it is imperative for you to find your own alternative solutions and to get them on the ballot, thus squelching the power of the industry associations to steal your democracy from you.

A one percent increase in payroll taxes, half of which are paid by the employer would put the Social Security problem to rest completely for at least fifty more years. It is already safe until the year 2042. This tax raise would make it solvent until the end of this century. If the situation worsens you could always look at it again with a further raise in taxes or a different solution that has become more creative and popular.

What is at stake in an issue like this is the basic fabric of your society and you must wake up to what they are really doing whenever they take away something that has worked so well for all these years. The Republican party and mostly due to its leader President Bush wants you to live in a society where the wealthiest people, the most successful people have absolutely no responsibility to care for those who are less fortunate.

Yet, it is the less fortunate, the hard working, humble people who give them their wealth and their success in the first place because of their hard work all their lives. From the basic interplay of these two kinds of people, the humble and the greedy, your system is created where some will succeed to a greater degree than most and some will always learn how to enjoy the fruits of your labor more than others. Is it fair that these lucky few should not have any regard for those who sacrificed so much for their success? I think not. The rich are always talking up the idea of "Giving Back to the Community". So, instead of just receiving lip service, this is a great way to force them to give back to the community every year. They should be ALL FOR IT.

Any social system that is going to last and remain democratic, must have at its base, a promise that everyone will participate in the freedom from want and need to a more or lesser degree. This requires that the most successful in society have an obligation to pay for this promise.'

Here's a side issue. An argument that should illustrate the DIRE NEED for National Ballot Measures before this country is totally destroyed by our elected leaders.

President Bush suggested and tried mightily to take the Social Security System and throw it to his cronies on Wall Street and let them invest all of the Social Security funds for all the retired Americans. Luckily, Bush, probably because he was distracted by his wrong-turn in Iraq trying to find weapons of mass-destruction, was not able to get this done.

If he had, ALL RETIRED AMERICANS TODAY would be out in the streets, because at the end of his administration, the stock market lost more than TEN TRILLION DOLLARS in EQUITY, and guess who's equity that would have been under Bush's little sneak attack on the senior citizens?

It is also very odd that the President has suggested that you take some of your money and invest it in the market in retirement plans. It's as if he was unaware that we already have that law on the books and they have been on the books for decades. Any American, since about 1980, can put money aside for their retirement and their health insurance, deducted from their income TAX FREE in plans known as I.R.A.'s (Individual Retirement Accounts) for anyone who is an employee and Keogh Plans for the Self Employed AND INVEST IT IN THE STOCK MARKET.

With National Ballot Measures in place – we could have either OVERTURNED and VETO'ED anything the CORRUPT and MORALLY BANKRUPT PRESIDENT BUSH or any other President no matter what they tried to force upon us. We could either propose something better than what the President has in mind OR just totally reject his ideas. I hope it's obvious to my readers that this power of the people will in the long run save this country both FINANCIALLY and MORALLY.

That leads me to another Great EXAMPLE of NATIONAL BALLOT MEASURES.

The requirement that any Presidential candidate have at a minimum a college degree with a B+ average or better in his or her college grades. That would have made the Presidency and all the power it contains unattainable by BUSH who had only a 'C' average in college and spent most of his time partying. And a 'C' average at YALE is really a FAILIING grade since they don't give anything lower than a 'C'.

And of course, when you have 'C' average or a FAILING leader, you are going to get a 'C' average or FAILING country. It's just like night follows day. And actually, we're currently getting an F in ECONOMICS because of Bozo's like Bush and Obama and all the damage they can do. It's really as simple as that. REMEMBER: I voted for and worked for Obama because he told the world that he was all about "Change we can believe in". I was fooled AGAIN.

In a true democracy, this is another example of how we cannot allow the concentration of so much power in the hands of such a small group of morally bankrupt people. To have the greatest country in the world run by a small group of pinheads, the PUNY and UNDERSIZED BRAINTRUST at a time when we have the TECHNOLOGY to use a much larger BRAINTRUST is just INSANITY of the worst kind.

And in case you believe that Congress has something to do with making the laws, remember, 90% of all Congress people are lawyers and what are lawyers trained to do in all the law schools? Represent Big Business because that's where the money is.

So, why do you put all lawyers in positions of making the laws? Because that's the only choice you get from the Two Party system, themselves, run by lawyers. Is this democracy? Is this a productive way to run the world? We have issues in this world that requires the best thinking of thousands of scientists, government people, consumers, technicians, programmers, doctors, lawyers, to solve some of the most difficult problems in history.

Many people with the greatest minds need to use them in concert to discuss and solve problems dispassionately and without religion dictating what the outcome of these deliberations shall be.'

Example #6: A Federal Law requiring that shareholders must approve any compensation package for the companies they own.

Debate: This is something they have already passed in Switzerland, the most financially sound country in the world.

How much money is enough? How can anyone be worth more than a million bucks a year? Not even Warren Buffet or Bill Gates can physically work more than 50 to 60 hours a week. What do these people do must be so highly paid? Giving them stock options now is different. I agree with that form of compensation to give your corporate leaders the incentive to do their best work. But salaries above one million bucks per year is a gross mismanagement of the corporation because those funds should be paid back to the investors.

This problem of excessive corporate executive compensation excess is probably the greatest threat to capitalism the world has ever known and is parasitic in nature. After all, any corporation that is financed through stock holders is owned by the stockholders, the investors who have taken great financial risk to make the company happen and expand.

Whenever any employee is paid over one million dollars per year, he is actually stealing money that by rights is due to the stockholders as a return on their investment and for taking the greatest risk. There is no risk to any employee who accepts a salaried position with any company and therefore, until the stockholders are paid, the employees, especially the chief executives, owe the stockholders as much money as they can in return for their investment above any salaries over a reasonable amount.

To do anything else in returning to the investors is fraudulent use of power. What happens in your present economy is that many greedy chief executives, and this has become an epidemic now, all conspire with their board members to grant themselves more and more money, to the detriment of the stockholders. No one person could possibly be worth more than a million dollars per year in compensation.

The conspiracy is very popular today in the corporate board rooms of America and unfortunately it encourages executives to try and wrestle as much money away from the stock holders as they can with total disregard for the long term health of their companies. Eventually, the companies who are being eaten alive by these parasites are forced into bankruptcy such as the Enron, Worldcom and NOW ALL OF WALL STREET FRAUD situations of the last few years.

None of the executives who steal this money has ever been forced to pay it back. Tens of thousands of jobs are lost when a major corporation is taken down by the parasites who ran them. And, competitors take over the field, making it extremely costly for the consumer as well whenever these companies fail. There are only forty or fifty hours per week that are available to any worker regardless of their positions. The rest of the time is spent sleeping, eating and enjoying life to some extent.

It is imperative for a just society that no one can earn in these allotted hours to more than a reasonable compensation for their service to their company, no matter who they are, or how talented. And, it's not like there is a shortage of talent. Tens of millions of American workers are just as qualified to run any corporation as any of these over-paid parasites. Many of the workers in the rank and file of these companies actually know more about the company and how to run it better than an outsider chosen for their celebrity at another corporation.

It's different, if someone were to invent something useful, or write a great song, create a really wonderful sculpture, painting, or other work of art or something that has a value greater than the time it took to create it. Working at a job, no matter what that job, should never constitute a greater return than what the stockholders are allotted.

Even the President of the United States, the single most stressing and most rewarding job there could be, is only allotted a few hundred thousand dollars a year and they don't seem to end up in poverty when they leave office. Far from it, they always seem to end up on easy street somehow. Let all executives live more modestly as the Chief Executive does.

There will be no shortage of talented and qualified applicants for these jobs, rest assured.' 'The main problem with society is that the rich get richer and the poor get poorer. It's a question of having a fair and EQUITABLE SOCIETY where there are no GREAT CHASMS OF INEQUALITY, jealousies, no class warfare.

In every corporation where there is an executive who are overpaid, there are tens of thousands of employees who are underpaid, barely able to pay their rent, living from day to day, finding it very difficult to pay for the bare essentials. They have no health care, poor nutrition, very little time for recreation, poor educational choices, all because the executives at the top are stealing money from them and the stockholders.

Is this the right kind of society for AMERICA GOING FORWARD? Is this the right thing to do with any corporation, an entity that is formed for the benefit of all who come in contact with it. Just because a corporation is no single individual, does not mean that it doesn't have a soul.

The purpose of the corporation is not for a few people to get rich, but to make it possible for the greatest number of people to prosper in society, and not just the stockholders.

IN SHORT, you cannot have a REAL DEMOCRACY in AMERICA until you are allowed to vote on issues like these few examples. With National Ballot measures we would be able to control our own destiny, create the right research for the right time, encourage other countries to emulate us. We can solve the problems of the day, quickly and efficiently without all the constant political bickering that we see every day on TV.

Here's a few more examples without much debate, but which are of obvious benefit to all.

Using Google SuperVote and National Ballot Measures we could easily and quickly -

1. Abolish the Electoral College
2. Prohibit any more Bank Bail Outs
3. Approve a Four Day Work Week
4. Require that all Freeways have modern Elevated MagLev Train tracks down the center for clean and efficient mass transit.
5. Shut Down the NSA.
6. Cut CIA Budget to 1 Billion per year.
7. Shut Down the DEPT of Homeland Security
8. Save Social Security by increasing withholding on all incomes, without limits.
9. Put Social Security back on its own separate part of the TREASURY UNTOUCHABLE by the Treasure for general expenditures.
10. Legalize Marijuana
11. IMMIGRATION reform.
12. ABOLISH the TRIP and FALL LAWSUITS
    (WE ALL PAY FOR THESE SCAM ARTISTS and lawyers who help them scam us.)
13. ABOLISH THE PERSONAL INCOME TAX AND REPLACE (MAYBE) WITH A NATIONAL SALES TAX THAT IS ALSO A GRADUATED SCALE THAT DISCOURAGES ENVIRONMENTALLY HARMFUL PRODUCTS

Food would be exempt: HOWEVER LUXURY FOODS like caviar and liquor would NOT be exempt. BUT BUYING A GAS GUZZLING CAR - IS TAXED AT say 25%. This would HELP PAY for the DAMAGE that these cars are doing to the planet. AND of course, over time, discourage their purchases until they go to ZERO because there will be ELECTRIC CARS encouraged by their EXEMPTION from this tax.

14. Limit the pensions of Federal Employees to no more than 100% of pensions in the Private Sector in similar Industries.
    We could even tackle Global Issues with the Google SuperVote-National Ballot Measures.

SO, Let's tackle the POISONING OF OUR OCEANS

Blocking MERCURY from Coal Fired Power Plants getting into the oceans because we need fish and other living things to prosper in the oceans or else we're going to suffocate from the lack of oxygen, which mostly comes from the marine eco-system.

15. FROM THIS DAY FORWARD any Power Plant using COAL to generate its power must PROVE to the EPA that their effluent is as clean or CLEANER than the air that went in or PAY A FINE equal to THEIR ENTIRE YEARLY PROFIT PER DAY of the infraction.

That would stop it - I guarantee it.

NOW, they're going to moan and groan and tell us all how this is impossible, but it's NOT, it's just an annoyance to their management. Instead of being able to go to their local country club and play golf three days a week, they'd have to cut it to TWO because they would need to spend an extra day at the office making sure that the scrubbers were put in place and operating correctly. SO, they either figure out a practical way to COMPLY with our laws OR they use something else like NAT GAS. Which is NOT polluting our oceans.

VERY SIMPLE FOLKS See how much fun we can have with Google Super Vote? JUST WATCHING THEM SQUIRM will be my favorite past time.

And they'll point to the poor coal miners in West Virginia who will lose their jobs. Could happen but do we really want to live in a world that forces people to work in Coal Mines?

AN ACCOMPANYING LAW could be to provide the FUNDING to get coal miners into college or better yet, a VOCATIONAL TRAINING in a new industry that is GOOD for the rest of us, like ELECTRIC CARS. We'll be needing millions of folks to work on the INFRASTRUCTURE for this clean form of Transportation. What better place to put the Coal Miners? DOING GOOD for the planet, instead of harm.

See how easy this process is of merely thinking creatively? Fun isn't it?

Unfortunately, Congress doesn't think this way because their vote is always for sale. And, they don't have enough money to bribe us all. Remember that important distinction, please.

They will try to influence us of course with their constant ADVERTISING

And this brings me to the coolest Google Super Vote-National Ballot Measure of all.

It would read as follows:

All Television Advertising must be distributed to the viewer in the

first two minutes of each hour of programming or in the last two minutes of the hour of programming. No advertisements of any kind are allowed in between these times, or during any show or production of any kind.

TV Advertising is actually SPAM. We didn't ask for it. They don't have a relationship with us. Yet we are forced to see it as it interrupts every TV Show on the air today unless it's a paid movie. Why do these advertisers have this power to interrupt us all, when I as a lone entrepreneur on the Internet who wants to advertise to people on the Internet and I can actually go to jail if I continue to do this.

The reason, I cannot SPAM and they can is because I'm just a little guy. I don't have a multi-million dollar Lobbying Budget so that I can tell Congress how to structure this economy.

AND this is why they can SPAM YOU and I cannot. IT was all determined by George W. Bush, in the ultimate BRIBERY of all time and one that started our country down the path of destruction, the minute that this man took office. Bush couldn't wait to get the Anti-Spam laws on the books. They purchased this man PRIOR to the election through his Republican Party Controllers.

So, in the first few days of his Administration, George W. Bush slammed through Congress, two laws that made it impossible for the little guy to compete against the large corporations who were his masters.

The Anti-Spam Act and the Do-Not-Call List. These two laws were jammed through Congress by George W. Bush in the first 90 days of his administration. Now, remember, when they want to try and solve most problems it takes them decades to debate it and attach so many amendments to the final bill that it is rendered totally bogus by the time it becomes law.

But, in these two laws, they were both passed without hearings in Congress and without debate and in only 90 days of Bush putting them together. Written by the large corporations, it changed the Internet so that no one can advertise to the masses without a huge budget, in other words THEM, by calling it SPAM, but THEY could still SPAM YOU ON TV and RADIO.

The little entrepreneur who was using the power of the Internet to compete with the large corporations were put to death, and this being the LIFE-BLOOD of a healthy economy - any good economist will tell you this - started us down the path of economic catastrophe that we all suffer now.

ONE MAIN AGAIN - The OPPOSITE of DEMOCRACY - George W. Bush again, that sneaky crook made it illegal TO COMPETE with the established corporations and why? Because he knew there would be a HUGE PAY-OFF for him and his family someday.

And, this was done by also allowing them more and more of your VIEWING TIME to SPAM YOU. You now have to watch about ONE-THIRD of your viewing time as Advertisements - SPAM.

While, the emails to you, of a SO-CALLED SPAMMER, a small business person trying to save you money on some goods or services he was marketing, would never have exceeded a fraction of a minute of your time, if you simply hit the delete button and/or had him filtered out of your inbox.

Now, I want to finish this chapter with a very sad story that involves one of our greatest Americans - Walt Disney, the founder of Disney Land and Disney World.

Way back in the 1950's Walt Disney could see the future. As he was making plans to build Disney Land, he came across something that we have all experienced in his parks - the Monorail. It whisks his visitors all over these parks in clean and quiet luxury. They do no harm to the environment because they are powered by electric motors that do not have any toxic gases going out into the atmosphere at all, not a single drop of toxic effluent ever.

Walt Disney could also see the area of Southern California booming like nothing else before. Soldiers were coming home from combat in World War Two and when they landed in Los Angeles or San Diego, they all fell in love with the warm climate - It never rains in Southern California - and the beauty of the area, which at that time was Hollywood and the rest was all orange groves, apple groves, walnut groves, peach groves, and like that everywhere that the eye could see.

So, Walt could also see that as people were immigrating into the area, they had no other form of transportation than cars, and so rapidly the area was forced to chop down all of this beautiful and pristine and clean farms and fields and turn them into freeways and roads for the cars.

It was just the beginning of this alarming trend, so Walt Disney spent his own money and tried to convince the area political leaders to build out the infra-structure of Southern California by using mostly the Monorail. They turned him down, because the corporate interests at the time, were GM, Ford, Chrysler, concrete contractors, and tire manufacturers and of course all they had to do to counter-act the more beneficial alternative of Monorails connecting all points of Southern California was to bribe these same officials - and they spent less than one million dollar to do just that which created the Southern California nightmare of traffic congestion and pollution that we all must suffer today if we live there or are just passing through.

This horrific example of how the greed for money is destroying the world is just a tiny microcosm of the larger example of how this country is run.

We have to establish a system where people like Walt Disney can put beautiful, highly beneficial and elegant solutions on the ballot so that the average citizen can decide. Because in our common wisdom, we know better than the people at the helm of our ship who are only interested in their own benefits - NOT YOURS or MINE.

CHAPTER EIGHT - The Grass Roots

This book was intended to start he New American Revolution. It's a peaceful one this time because there are no foreign boots on our soil, not yet. There is a presence of evil from within that we must defeat and we must defeat it with the same ardor and bravery that we saw in the original founders of this great nation. As such, YOU, my readers are the Co-Founders of the next version of America, America 2.0, Inc. It is incumbent upon all of YOU, the readers of this book to do something now that you have the blueprint for change in front of you. To that end, we have given you all the ammunition that you may require. We have given you the procedure for regaining control of this government and we have given you the rationale.

You need only to take a the first step by aligning your life's journey with the life journey's of your compatriots. By joining in the new alternative Economy, suggested herein and amplified on our web site. you have the path completely open. The first step involves only in the acceptance that your life must be dedicated to this cause and that it can be dedicated to this cause simply by creating the will to do so.

The fact that there are others willing to take up the cause with you is an assurance that will grow and grow and eventually there will be a greater safety in our numbers than in the numbers of those who oppose this historic change. Using Grass Roots Capitalism may be accepted by the Obama Administration. Watch for developments at WHITEHOUSE.GOV As of the writing of this edition, President Obama proclaimed that he is interested in hearing from citizens in what he called it, the CITIZEN'S BRIEFING BOOK but it has since evolved to The White House Petitions.

UPDATE: As soon as Obama saw that the people wanted to pass IDEAS like the ones that I've shown you in the PREVIOUS CHAPTER - he TOOK DOWN this web site.

THUS again proving to the world that they are NOT INTERESTED IN REAL DEMOCRACY at all.

I leave the rest of this chapter intact so you can see how we were on the right path UNTIL someone who's really in charge of this country TOLD THE WHITE HOUSE TO STOP promoting Real Democracy.

We have created a Web Site to interact with the White House Petitions by proposing some NEW IDEAS that we don't see coming from our Government people any time soon. So, please VISIT this website and SIGN one or more of our PETITIONS as part of the Process of gaining total Democracy.

Here at The White House Web Site, any citizen can submit ideas that he or she thinks the President should see. The ideas are submitted to the community and they are voted UP or DOWN by other users of the system. The best proposals are to be given to the President in the form of a Daily Briefing from the Citizens. This system could be used to achieve many of the goals and concepts first proposed in this book. We're hoping that our readers will use this REAL DEMOCRACY avidly and encourage the President to work on making more of our ideas a realty. We're impressed with President Obama's Democracy Instincts thus far and we all want to encourage him to continue down this path.

Later, President Obama announced that he will be extending his Grass Roots Organization to extend and expand on supporting his administration. We believe that this unprecedented notion as also inspired by this book and our web sites. No other President has ever shown the least interest in Real Democracy and we have been rebuffed by every President during the last 50 years, until Number 44, President Obama. He has not endorsed this concept yet, however, we are confident that he will given enough interest from the public and especially fellow Democrats.

ISN'T IT TIME FOR SOME REAL CHANGE? IF YOU DO NOT TAKE THEM UP ON THEIR MODEST OFFERS OF REAL CHANGE AND HELP PROMOTE IT – WE WILL NEVER be safe. So GO to PetitonForAmerica.com and give Real Democracy in America at least a minute or two of your time. Give it a few minutes MORE to TELL EVERYONE YOU KNOW. Put our BOOK on your WEB SITE, put the URL to link it inside EVERY EMAIL in your signatures. Call people and tell them you're going to send them a copy of the book. POST it as a COMMENT on all the political blogs. Post it continually in your FaceBook and/or Twitter, Quora, Pinterest, LinkedIn, Google+ accounts. Make YOUTUBE VIDEOS about the book. Do all of this and MORE and keep the pressure up for REAL CHANGE.

We must have no illusions, it will not be easy. This privatization of a government has never been tried before. But, when you look at all the earlier forms of government and how much they fail their own citizens with high unemployment, great disparity between the rich and the poor, faulty education, bankrupt social programs, corruption, economic chaos, etc, the argument for doing something completely different becomes more and more real. We must remember that any path to Socialism is a dark and desolate path from which very few nations of any historic import have ever returned.

We can return, but only if we act quickly before we have gone too far. The Fascists of Nazi Germany took over the Banks FIRST. Then, they took over all of the rest of Industry and made them build more and more weapons until World War was the inevitable conclusion.

The Military Industrial Complex of this nation has already been infiltrated by the Lobbyists who wouldn't care if we went into a Third World War, even though World War III would spell the end of humanity and most other forms of life on this planet. The mass extinction of species is something that has happened on this planet many times before, but in every instance that we know of, the causes were natural ones. In this case, it will be Man-Made.

This will doom our civilization to eternal damnation if we allow it. We must not and can not allow it. You MUST take the action of dismantling the old power system of greed and corruption that has plagued this great nation and replace it in the manner of TRUE

DEMOCRACY, real democracy where the rights of the shareholders are superior to all other privileges in society.

We must use the new form of Controlled Capitalism or what I call, Grass Roots Corporatism to grow a prosperous world out of the needs of people to survive and lead healthy, productive and profitable lives. Only a form of Capitalism that super-cedes the Government can work to achieve all this. This may come as a surprise to my readers, but I personally cannot do this alone.

We will need the support of MILLIONS of AMERICANS to agree to adopt this REVOLUTIONARY CHANGE in the way that we do our political and economic business. Therefore, we ask that you yourself get on board and then begin to bring your friends and associates over with you. The GOOD NEWS is that we have designed a very simple way to HELP you SPREAD the WORD and make converts to the cause of Freedom and Democracy in America.

And, I have put forth here the STEPS that need to be taken and in the order that they will need to be taken.

STEP ONE: Spread this knowledge around. Help publish this Book far and wide. This eBook must go Viral, which means as you help create readers, we share the PROFITS with YOU, our readers.

STEP TWO: JOIN in the Discussion. BLOG the world with your ideas on this topic. JOIN US on QUORA where the discussion is continuing in a purely democratic fashion.
http://quora.com/MichaelMathiesen

Go to some of my BOARDS and CONTRIBUTE to new ways that we have installed for our readers to SUPPORT themselves and SUPPORT this new concept at the same time. We are so blessed in this country to have as much as we have. We are going down in terms of our position in the world and in our ability to serve up the American Dream right now, but we can turn it around and we must turn it around. We have so much to be thankful for and we need to START HERE and UNITE on the one truly NEW IDEA that cannot fail to improve the lives of us all in the most equitable manner.

Above all, we must remember from where we came. Around three thousand years ago, when most of humanity were still living in caves and eating anything that walked past, there was a group of people in Ancient Greece who began to build the beautiful Grecian Temples like the Parthenon that we are so familiar with today and which is still standing in Athens. The people of Greece got the amazing idea that they should rule themselves through a new system of order they called, "Democracy", literally meaning in Greek, 'the People Rule'.

This was revolutionary for its day. Up until this time, for tens of thousands of years, most people on Earth were ruled by harsh tyrants, princes and kings who ruled over them with vicious unconcern for the welfare of what they considered to be the lower working classes. The Ancient Greeks, living in their splendid buildings that have yet to be duplicated, even after all this time, would use their new technology to POLL themselves on all their most urgent problems and the best proposed solutions. A group of riders would set out on horseback a few weeks before election day and they would post the latest STATE PROPOSITIONS.

In those days, they would ask their citizens if they wanted to join the equivalent of the United Nations, the Peloponnesian League, a mutual defensive group of city-states who would come to the defense of one another when the Persians attacked. They might be asking the citizens if they wanted to raise their own taxes or put a sales tax on Olives to generate enough revenues to build schools or roads.

The entire city-state, not more than 20 or 30 miles in diameter, the horsemen could post the propositions in a few days. They would gather round in the sunny village squares and discuss these propositions amongst themselves and they would patiently listen to the pros and cons of each proposition, with many times, tempers flaring and the debates became heated and passionate discussions on either side.

Then, a few days later, they would take a vote. Each citizen would take up a small pebble, either black or white and place them into a large pot. White stood for YES and black stood for NO. With more WHITE pebbles than BLACK, the PROPOSITION passed and vice versa, if there were more BLACK pebbles.

This form of government – THE FIRST REAL DEMOCRACY in the world lasted for many more years than modern America has existed. The people were the happiest they have ever been in terms of equality and cultural appreciation. This idea was so popular that it caught on all over the Mediterranean, although altered significantly when the Roman Empire conquered Greece and

Democracy was stifled and controlled by the Roman Republic, really just a poor imitation of the Greek invention.

But, then over the next two thousand years, the idea remained in the hearts and minds of the greatest thinkers of the world and slowly but surely, the seed of democracy was fertilized with new energy and re-invigorated after the long period known as the Dark Ages, democracy flowered once more in Europe and then finally And, luckily for all of us in the modern age, the Internet has came across the ocean to bless the fledgling United States of America.

As we have seen, it grew and strengthened through the constant nurturing of our beloved Constitution given to us so generously by the founding fathers of this great nation. Over time, this democracy became the greatest nation on the Earth, the strongest the most powerful determined bunch of folks the world had ever known. We breathe free today because many millions of us gave their lives for the concept of freedom and liberty, so carefully nurtured over the centuries like a flame that we could not let die out.

Cautiously now, we are at the point where the flame of freedom it is flickering once again because we have leadership who have not truly been interested in the problem2s of the people in the villages and they have remained in their temples of conceit, arrogance and incompetence and tried to rule the world, when it is their duty to manage this country, not others.

But, this is why Democracy was invented, to CONTROL the inadequacies of the TOO FEW who sit on high and try to dictate with their tiny brains what is wrong and what is right. become the LIVING PROOF that democracy is the most powerful force on Earth for good.

The Internet is democracy as represented by the millions of computers and wires and processors, keyboards, monitors, servers, etc. that make up the almost limitless connections of people that we now know as the Internet. Each node on the World Wide Web is connected to a living, breathing, thinking animal. The sum total of all that thought, all our daily work goes into what we learn and decide on the Web in mass communication every day.

None of this could happen if it weren't for the force of democracy working through the many millions of us who desire to live in a world that is decentralized and free of the burdens that the central authorities want to impose on us more and more. And, in the beginning, even the Internet was just a hodge-podge of a few Main Frame computers that sat in large rooms of the major corporations. Big Iron, they called them a few years back, but then through the beauty of evolution, these first master computers grew smaller and smaller and cheaper until almost every family in the country could afford one or even more than one.

Then we connected them to each other over our phone lines and the rest is history. This miraculous technological evolution could only have taken place in a democratic society where the government was not strong enough or willing enough to prevent it from happening, as they have tried to do in China and Russia. The force of democracy is so great that even there, the Internet could not be crushed entirely.

In these Communist countries they block the people from gaining access to sites that refute what the governments are telling them, but the people find a way to get the truth anyway and these links of truth and reason and freedom are going to strengthen and grow firm in the nervous system of the planet more and more just as our brains grow by developing our networks of synapses and axons of fleshy grey matter.

Democracy is really the will of the society at large and this will becomes stronger and more intelligent as it becomes more aware of itself and its environment. This awareness of self is human consciousness at work and consciousness is the force that created the Universe. It's the most powerful force in the universe and it is part of every living cell in our bodies and in every atom and every molecule of the Earth, the Sun, the Moon, and all the stars in heaven. Consciousness never rests, it never gives up on us. It never releases its hold on reality and it never stops growing. It cannot be thwarted by the puny little selfish minds of tyranny and authority. It cannot be deterred. We can take temporary losses, as we have done during the years of the Bush Administration and when we don't fight this kind of corruption at the highest level, then there is of course NO HOPE.

We have to BREAK the BACK of APATHY because the George W. AMBUSH's of the world USE that to KEEP US ENSLAVED.

We are at a crossroads today. We can blow ourselves all panic and ignore our own power in our collective mind-power. But, eventually, sanity is restored and we win even over the most brutal of beasts. It is inexorable. It is inevitable that we will win in the end.

Truth is far more powerful than lies and fraud. It is more powerful because Truth is innate in all of us. It's in our DNA. It's been around since the Big Bang and Truth will be around even after the universe dies out forever. We are all connected to it now and so Truth is more powerful today than at any other time in history. Truth can never be defeated for long. It can be confused at times as they who hate the Truth do their best to weaken the signal, put out too much static and diversion. But as long as we maintain our confidence in ourselves there is nothing they can do that will defeat us or slow us down for long. to smithereens or we can start to lay down the foundation for a New World based on peace, brotherhood and understanding.

There is no reason why we must hate anyone anywhere else in the world. There is no reason for them to hate us as long as we show them the way to democracy and freedom and prosperity as we have known it, experienced it, enjoyed it. Why should anyone suffer on this planet? Why should we have so many wars and so much poverty and despair? There is no reason for this except that our leaders keep us bickering so much that they fool us into thinking that we must hate our enemies. They keep us so plugged up with fear and paranoia because they know that if the world were run well, if all things were managed properly, we would not need them.

They would have to take the kinds of jobs that we perform daily and this frightens them to death because they hate to work, hate to have to think creatively. They take no pride in a day's work well done. They have no interests in anything except their own power, their own authority over us. When we have finally established America 2.0, Inc, as the most powerful successor to the First Version of the good ole USA, then the rest of the world will have to stand up and take notice. They will all know that there is a new brand of America around, one based on peace and prosperity and understanding.

With the power of the Internet and Real Democracy we can begin to share our knowledge, power and equity with the rest of the planet. We can show them how to fish, how to farm, how to live in such a way that the entire planet can sustain those of us who live here. Democracy was in less than 1 tenth of one percent of overall world population at the time, but somehow, this scrappy determined little nation had their culture copied all over the world and over the next two thousand years Democracy finally caught hold in North America at just the right time, when this country was being formed.

And, with the power of democracy, we became the strongest and most admired nation on the Earth. The Internet is the proof of everything we are saying about DEMOCRACY. The Internet is the MOST DEMOCRATIC TOOL in the history of the world. We have EVENED out the PLAYING FIELD amongst home based businesses, because on the Internet, you can reach millions of people without any advertising costs and Social Networking Sites have made this all the more beneficial and easy for any small business person.

The distribution of this book is one great example of the democratization of the Internet. Without it, I could not have had the impact that we are having on the Public. THEREFORE, it is very appropriate that we should use it for REAL DEMOCRACY in our political and economic system.

STEP THREE: GO TO: www.America2inc.com - To Get an UPDATE on everything we're doing and finding successful.

Some final thoughts on this chapter The TWO-PARTY adversarial System doesn't work any more because the greed of all the people involved. It's obvious to even the casual observer that the Two-Party system has devolved into a new kind of despotism where Americans are ruled over by the Party elite, the Lobbyists and Special Interest Groups.

It's not enough to vote in a new batch of crooks. We have to change the SYSTEM that allows this to happen. Here's why. Take a look at what is happening in America right at this moment. This is a snapshot of American Democracy in Action right now. As we speak, President Obama is bailing out the major banks because they don't have enough money to stay afloat. If they fail, it would produce a ripple effect that would cost the American economy billions and billions of dollars.

And please remember this because I have obviously favored one side of the political spectrum over another in this book and in talks that I give, but that is ONLY because UNTIL we get a better system, we have to INCH toward real CHANGE, by favoring the group that gives us a little bit more positive change than the other side. It's a matter of pragmatism that we must all use as wisely and carefully as we can.

But, make no mistake the Two-Party System is a CONSPRACY against the average citizen. Deep down, they care about their OWN INTERESTS ahead of anyone else. Bush was the WORST example of this and the proof is that he didn't go after Osama Bin Laden, the worst INVADER this country has ever had, BECAUSE the BUSH FAMILY has BUSINESS INTERESTS with the SAUDI's and even the Bin Laden FAMILY.

This conflict of interest should have been a major scandal much bigger than WaterGate or anything else in history, but alas, the traitor seems to have gotten away with TREASON. That's why I tend to favor one side over the other in my own mind. One half of the TWO-PARTY CONSPIRACY is the worst half and we can gain some progress by banishing the folks who bring us this kind of scandalous and treasonous behavior over and over again.

Nixon was a Traitor in my book because he was a SERIAL MURDERER who completely TRASHED the reputation of the greatest country in the world. Can we really make this claim any more? When Bush COPIES NIXON by invading IRAQ, it helps answer that question. Hundreds of thousands of innocent Iraqi's killed by our bombs and over 5,000 of our own heroes sent to the deaths, with hundreds of thousands more losing an arm, a leg or an eye, because Bush wanted to punish Saddam Hussein for trying to assassinate his father.

Well, I would have applauded BUSH if he had used his own money or his own personal security forces to kill his family's personal enemy - Saddam. But, he used TWO TRILLION DOLLARS of YOUR MONEY and MINE to do this and used thousands of innocent lives to kill Saddam Hussein and the TREASONOUS part of my indictment is that he really should have spent these resources to kill OSAMA BIN LADEN, not Saddam Hussein.

How can one that is supposed to be a leader lead his devoted soldiers to their deaths for such a reason as this? How can anyone sleep at night having sent over 5,000 of his most loyal soldiers to their death and disfiguration for such a charade, knowing clearly that there were no weapons of mass destruction in Iraq and yet he was able to send these finest of Americans to their deaths without any second thoughts. This is not the kind of leadership that America needs nor deserves. We deserve and need far better than this. In the next version of America, there is hope that we will finally grow up as a nation and take our country to the next level.

What do we learn from this? We learn that it's human nature for any political force to always want to be in power and that they have no real core values, they just believe whatever they know from doing market research that the people want to hear at any given time in order for them to get into power. It's like water always flowing downhill. Water cannot flow uphill. That's impossible and we never see rivers flowing uphill.

Water always flow downhill because of gravity and the nature of water to follow the greatest forces of nature. Gravity forces the water in mountains to wind up in the oceans and that's if the water doesn't evaporate on the way to the ocean where it ends up falling on the mountains again and then flowing to the ocean. Water always ends up in the ocean no matter what other interruptions there may be from conflicting forces such as evaporation. So, it is with politicians.

In order to enjoy their profession to the fullest, they must be in power. They must have a pulpit from which to spout off and impress others. So, no matter what core beliefs they may have internally, we never learn what they are, because they will follow the path of least resistance, political gravity into their highest position of power, even though most of them are not qualified to be in charge of anything. So, for this very scientific piece of human nature that is immutable and cannot be in dispute, the two-party system doesn't work. Add to this the very hideous effect of money on the Two-Parties and now you see how insidious it is for us to have two-parties one in power and the other not in power.

The money forces of the country will be used to put the opposing party in office. The money being the lobbyists, those who represent big business interests. The money pushes the party out of office into office again. This is necessary because the party in power requires more money to stay in power than the party that is out of power. So, supply and demand takes over and the party out of power is paid to get back in. It's a vicious cycle that repeats itself over and over in American politics. We see it again and again and there is only one solution to break this cycle of dependence on deceit, treachery and lies. We must have a THIRD BALANCING FORCE, one in the middle of these two adversaries so that the THIRD WAY can play one party against the other sort of playing up to them until one or the other makes an alliance with the CORE VALUES of that third party and thus create a MAJORITY that cannot be broken. Then, and only then, can COMMON SENSE PREVAIL in this country again.

THAT THIRD FORCE must be the ordinary middle class folks, and we must get to this position by TAKING STOCK in our own country, literally becoming the MAJOR SHAREHOLDERS. Thus, the power of the PEOPLE to rule their own country is assured by our equity position in the country, an equity position much greater than any single political party or business interest. By Incorporating the United States Government, a quick and simple process of amending the Constitution as we have seen in previous chapters, we create a Third Party instantly that is the perfectly balancing THIRD FORCE in this country, the Power of the People, the common stock shareholders of America, the people who invest their blood seat and tears in this country every day, few of whom are paid back in anything except a paycheck that can be interrupted at any time without warning, their families to be thrown away like so much trash.

By allowing everyone to own stock in America, this disenfranchisement, this disgraceful class warfare will be finally over and every man, woman and child in this country will have a Net Worth. Not all Net Worth will be equal, but at least we can live in a society where everyone has an equal chance at owning at least part of their country and with a little hard work, education, training and diligence, any American citizen can get a fair shake, a fair chance at the American Dream. There is no reason why we should not all have a comfortable retirement.

There is no reason why all of our children should not have access to a college education. There is no reason why we should not all have a roof over our heads with plenty to eat. The only reason, these resources are distributed so unfairly, so unequally in this country is because we have not had a better way to think about our economy.

We have used tired worn-out formulas that do not work any longer. We've tried outright capitalism. We've tried pure socialism. The human race has suffered mightily under despotism, monarchies, Communist states and everything else imaginable under the sun. BUT, we have never tried a system of 'Pop Corporatism' where everyone has a shot of owning a piece of the rock and is given a piece of the rock to get started.

THIS IS AMERICA 2.0, Inc – Taking Stock in America would do. It would be the greatest political and social experiment in the history of the world and we have nothing to lose at this point in giving it a shot. Certainly the alternative of allowing people like George W. AMBUSH to gain control of our destiny and do to any future generation what he did to this one is totally unacceptable and must be insured against ever happening again.

When this country was attacked on 9/11 by nineteen young Saudi and other Arab religious fanatics armed only with box cutters, very few of us could have predicted that this act of terrorism would cost us our entire CAPITALIST structure. IF the terrorists were trying to wreck our entire economy by driving an airplane or two into the World Trade Center, the financial capital of our country, they would not have succeeded in this, UNLESS they had lots more help.

It would take thousands more bureaucrats and politicians to HELP THEM in their ATTACK on our economy and it would also take them just SEVEN MORE YEARS. Osama Bin Laden is having the TIME OF HIS LIFE, laughing and scoffing and joking about America because OUR LEADERS gave him the VICTORY that is not seen or spoken or written about in thousands of years of History and folklore.

Our LEADERS have made Osama Bin Laden, the greatest folk hero of all time, bigger than Robin Hood or Paul Bunyan or Davy Crockett, or any other folk hero you care to name, because with this band of 19 men armed with box cutters, Osama Bin Laden was able to TAKE DOWN the ECONOMY, not only of the United States, but of all Western Christian Nations on one September Morning, and what's worse, he has lived to tell and brag about it since.

We spent TRILLIONS of DOLLARS and gave THOUSANDS of LIVES over TEN YEARS to help RUIN our economy. This is aiding and abetting the enemy, in my book at the very least and

TREASON at the worst. At least OBAMA finally got him. At least that's what they told us. There were no pictures of the final operation to kill Bin Laden and that is quite troubling to me. Could it be, Osama was already dead of his kidney disease and/or his wounds? It's suspicious to me that the Obama Administration refused to publish pictures of the operation. All we ever got was pictures of OBAMA and friends watching TV. They could have been watching a baseball game.

In a free and democratic society, openness and full disclosure, holding no secrets of our citizens is crucial to our long-term survival as a free and democratic society. Only 'Pop Corporatism' can deliver on this promise.

CHAPTER NINE – Can Government Ever Make a Profit?

ANSWER: NOT UNDER a NON-PROFIT money losing form of organization - NEVER. This is a prescription for failure only. Take the United States Post Office for example. They currently lose about 8 BILLION DOLLARS PER YEAR and the difference is funded by – Guess Who? Yes, you and me. Federal Express, on the other hand, MAKES 8 BILLION PER YEAR IN PROFITS.

SUGGESTION: Shut down the US Postal Service and HIRE Federal Express to deliver all our mail. Save the taxpayers 8 Billion Dollars per year in one simple change. So simple, isn't it now? But you see, a Losing Not-For-Profit Government does not have any incentives to stop losing money and that's the essence of our problems not only here in the USA but this philosophy is shared by most governments all over the world. I hope you see that this new Revolution could sweep the world and save it. We only have to begin it here. So, let's get down to it. So, here's one shining and SIMPLE thing the government could do to start making a profit from one of its essential services.

If you or I were President, we could accomplish this with ONE STROKE of the PEN. An executive order. DONE. BUT, instead, we have to wait until the bureaucrats can all think this decision over for DECADES before anything is done and the total cost of the MIS-MANAGEMENT can run into the TRILLIONS. This is JUST ONE EXAMPLE of the inefficiency and insanity in our government system. I could go through EVERY GOVERNMENT AGENCY and show you why they lose money and how to make them all PROFITABLE.

Imagine a government system with NO RED INK? Completely in the BLACK year after year and PAYING YOU AND ME, the citizens DIVIDENDS instead of holding out the cup asking us for MANDATORTY donations – TAXES - every time we turn around.

Why do we have to do things this way?

In a word – BUREAUCRACY – the most evil concept ever invented by Mankind. One organization, your government run Post Office has no one in charge that is telling the workers how to make a profit and there is no one in charge that knows how to make a profit.

US Postal Service administrators in the THOUSANDS, people who never deliver a single piece of mail to anyone in their entire careers, somehow find the time on our dime to go to fancy resorts in Hawaii and the Bahamas for FREE and spend thousands of dollars every day using Taxpayer Pre-Paid Credit Cards.

They only work enough to make it to age 50 where they can retire on 75% of Salary. If they have the guts, they hang on doing nothing until age 55 where they can retire on 90% Salaries. They get these Golden Retirement plans because NO ONE CARES. The entire philosophy of government when they realize how much money their losing is that NO ONE CARES.

And, they're right in the fact that no one in Government CARES. The taxpayer cares that all of this money is wasted, but we taxpayers have NO REPRESENTATION IN GOVERNMENT where they will watch out for our money. So, in the NOT-FOR-PROFIT scheme of things, NO ONE CARES really, no one who matters to the big spenders.

So, they NATURALLY feel ethically and morally bound to spend more and more and waste more and more of our money, simply because there is no supervision from anyone anywhere in government. AND it's PART OF THEIR CULTURE. It's in their DNA as bureaucrats. This is what they TEACH them in the COLLEGES and UNIVERSITIES in the Public Works Disciplines. HOW TO LOSE MORE TAXPAYER DOLLARS every year to KEEP THEIR JOBS.

Oh yes, the politicians make fancy speeches about controlling our government, but only when they need us to vote for them. Once they're in office, they say, "WHO CARES?" And, once again, they are right. No one cares who is in control of them at this point. We can control the campaigns of these people to some extent, but BOTH PARTIES are the same.

At the time of writing this edition of this book, one lonely Senator, Jim Bunning, from Kentucky is holding up Unemployment Insurance Payments to MILLIONS of people who are out of work by simply OBJECTING on the floor of the Senate. By Senate Rules, this is allowed, so my question is WHERE WERE THE OBJECTIONS to the BUSH WAR BILLS that wasted TRILLIONS OF OUR tax dollars? You're telling me that not ONE DEMOCRAT THOUGHT ABOUT OBJECTING and HOLDING UP THE WASTEFUL ACTIONS OF A CRIMINAL PRESIDENT? MORE BUREAUCRATIC BUNGLING in my book, but with a PARTISAN TWIST. Both parties do this.

NO, the two parties are really ONE. The difference is only in style. Think about it for a minute. How is it possible to lose 8 BILLION DOLLARS sending carriers around to every home and business in America every day delivering their mail? It's not possible to lose money at this, WHEN you're A MONOPOLY unless you're TRYING to GO BROKE.

Get the point? In a NOT for PROFIT business model, it's accepted, even rewarded when you LOSE money. If you made money by some accident, they'd think you're a bit odd and send you away.

BUT, in a FOR PROFIT ORGANIZATION it would be the rule of the day to MAKE MONEY and all you'd have to do is RAISE the FEES for your service or LAY PEOPLE OFF, or BOTH in order to show a profit to your Corporate Headquarters. The difference is really just one of adopting the right MIND SET. If you're in a FOR PROFIT environment, by Gosh and by Golly, somehow, managers will figure out a way to show a profit at their endeavors or be sent packing.

In a NOT FOR PROFIT environment, it's just the reverse. For any organization with a MONOPOLY on picking up the mail, putting it into trucks and airplanes and getting it to its proper destination, with no competitors and 40 CENTS per ounce, it should be a PIECE OF CAKE to make money at delivering mail.

INSTEAD, they work very very hard to LOSE BILLIONS EACH YEAR. And as bureaucrats they are UNMATCHED anywhere in the world if you want to call this a measure of SUCCESS. I don't. I call this a measure of our FAILURE TO CONTROL THEM.

The thought of our Government making a profit instead of losing our collective shirts every month may be very alien to many people. But, when you think about it, why should our government be pre-conditioned to lose our money every month? It's only such a long standing tradition for our government to do this, that today, it seems like the natural course of events. But it doesn't have to be that way and it really should NOT be that way.

All we have to do is think about it as a nation and make some basic philosophical changes to our consciousness on this topic and then it will seem like Cave Men were running the government in the old days when they didn't know any better and were so driven to spend more than they take in every year.

There are only two main issues when you focus on this subject. The revenue side of government activities, in other words, taxes, fees and impounds. And there's the expense side, the money that government spends for the common benefit, things like Unemployment Insurance, Social Security, Medicare, Defense, Regulation, that sort of thing.

The phrase I'm coining here - 'POP CORPORATISM' is all about the Government Making a Profit as they deliver the services that a good and booming society requires such as a RETIRMENT PLAN that is equitable and secure, roads, hospitals, schools, bridges, national security, a clean environment and protection for the Earth, safe food to eat, clean water to drink, clean air to breathe and enough energy to keep the whole thing growing in a complete holistic and ecological way that the world can emulate and humanity can survive and evolve into the long term future.

But how do we accomplish all this easily and simply and in a way that is acceptable to all stakeholders?

We're going to talk about the revenue side further on in this chapter where we show how to eliminate the Income Tax and convert it to a Consumption Tax. But, this first section, we need to look at the expenditure side, because it is the most egregiously wrong platform of ideas that we base our government upon that makes our proposal so much of a common sense one. We spend all of the government's revenues from the agencies that form the Federal Bureaucracy. Everyone knows the biggest ones, the Dept. of Defense with about 500 Billion in Budget per year.

With that money they contract for bombers and ships that cost in the BILLIONS of dollars EACH to make. They spend it on supporting our soldiers in all of our foreign adventures, Iraq, soon Iran, Afghanistan, South Korea and soon North Koreas, Germany even 50 years after World War II has some 50,000 of our troops stationed there, presumably in case Adolph Hitler really isn't dead and returns to power, they can take a shot at him and stop any further bloodshed? I don't know. I do know that the Dept. of Defense says that it costs about ONE MILLION DOLLARS per soldier to keep them equipped and in the field per year.

Want a truly efficient way to SPEND ALL OUR MONEY FOOLISHLY? Just look at what the Dept of Defense does for us all and at what cost.

That means our soldiers sitting around in Germany waiting for Hitler to come back to life is around FIFTY BILLION DOLLARS per YEAR of our tax dollars to defend against a guy that is obviously dead for fifty years.

We've all read the stories about the $50,000 toilet seats, the $100,000 wrenches, the $50 nails. The FIFTY MILLION DOLLAR AIRPLANES. The TEN BILLION DOLLAR SUBMARINES. So, there is not much doubt in most Americans' minds that there is HUGE WASTE, FRAUD and ABUSE in the Dept. of Defense alone.

In the Viet Nam War it ended up costing the American taxpayer about $100,000 per enemy soldier killed. I used to think that was the most horrible and wasteful abuse of our Government in my lifetime. HOWEVER George W. AMBUSH decided to break all records. These Viet Nam Kill Costs were a total bargain compared to the cost of a dead enemy in Iraq – over TEN BILLION PER KILL.

Then, there's the agencies that were created to look after the Environment, the EPA. There's the Agency that was created to look after America's Energy needs, the Dept. of Energy. There's the Dept. of Transportation was created to look after our Transportation needs.

There's the Dept. of Health and Human Services that was created to look after our Health Care needs and the list of agencies goes on and on. There are at least ONE HUNDRED of these entities that we can start to think of as DIVISIONS within the Corporate Government.

And, if you start to think of them as Divisions of the corporation, then you should then come to the question of WHY DON'T WE REQUIRE that all of our Corporation's Divisions be required to make a profit. In other words, stick within their budget and even raise some funds from their operations to help pay for some portion of their budget, if not all of it?

Let's take the Dept. of Energy. They could easily be reformed under 'Pop Coporatism' to start acting more like a Division of the Corporation and report to the CEO their profits, or losses each year. Whenever they make a huge loss, the CEO would then take the appropriate action and in the case of a real Corporation, that division head who continually loses money is FIRED and a new one when found who can turn around that errant division so that it makes a profit would be hired. See how thi8s works? Really simply common sense and old-fashioned business management techniques. This is NOT ROCKET SCIENCE, is it?

The Dept. of Energy is in charge of the research and development of new energy sources so that America could one day replace foreign oil as our main energy source. You mean to tell me that when your division is in charge of finding new energy sources and none are actually found, we can't change that forlorn situation? How DO THEY STAY IN BUSINESS? Simple – They're not interested in helping the country that has PAID them, sustained them all those years. They only make enough noise to make it look like they're accomplishing something. Yeah Sure. Like the Solar Company Solyndra that was given FIVE HUNDRED MILLION dollars by the Dept of Energy and then they IMMEDIATELY upon getting our money – used it to PAY OFF all the executives with OUR MONEY and filed for BANKRUPTCY. Does anyone get fired for this fiasco? NO.

On the PLUS SIDE if we look real hard - The Dept. of Energy should use its immense influence in the University Research community to find and locate some of the most talented researchers and subsidize them so that they can be free to find the energy sources of the FUTURE. THEN, the DOE could patent this new energy source and LICENSE IT TO INDUSTRY, thus making a profit on all its operations.

In this way, we can force this DEPT to make a profit and actually benefit the country to boot. There is a professor of

Electrical Engineering at the University of Missouri, for just one example, who has promising research on making batteries from Nuclear Radiation. The nuclear radiation is so low, it is less than background radiation we already have all around us, so it is not the kind of nuclear power we have to fear, yet the energy density, the POWER produced PER POUND of material contained in this battery is TEN TIMES GREATER than current battery technology and promises to be ONE HUNDRED TIMES GREATER with more research and development.

The Dept. of Energy should subsidize this fellow's research and when it becomes commercially viable, patent it, put it out for general consumption, take bids from battery and car manufacturers and make a PROFIT from its widespread usage in society, which is inevitable, given the current lack of energy alternatives and the great need in this world for cheap and clean electricity.

Believe it or not, the DOE does NOT act in this manner currently. Yes, they fund research, but they then allow the researcher to KEEP his patents or the UNIVERSITY he works for depending on his contract, and the Government, YOU AND ME, the real investors in this research GET NOTHING but BIG FAT GOOSE EGGS every year from the DOE and every other agency of the US Government.

IF AMERICA were set up as a Corporation, then this would change and every DIVISION within the corporation would have as its overall mission the requirement to make a profit. Then, we could PAY our citizens every year in DIVIDENDS, instead of STEALING MONEY from us every year so that THEY can merrily go along in their jobs with no real responsibility, other than picking up their pay checks every two weeks and making nice speeches.

The Dept of Transportation and the EPA have the same problem. They were set up to bring us newer and more efficient ways to move people about the planet, yet they have NEVER brought about any change in that regard and instead allow the Car Manufacturers continue to produce nothing but GAS GUZZLING CARS that use foreign oil and this is a major reason we are not a great nation any more.

In JAPAN and most of EUROPE they have trains that go over 300 MILES PER HOUR. No one is ever injured or killed. And, trains compete very well with Jet Planes that are extremely harmful to the environment. Jet exhaust, known as contrails, and you see them every day in the sky over your head, are responsible for GLOBAL DIMMING. Far less sunlight hits our farms and homes as a result of the CLOUD COVER that jet planes produce and is the main reason our winters have gotten so cold, EVEN THOUGH GLOBAL WARMING, the other effect of INTERNAL COMBUSTION ENGINES would produce the opposite effect, warming winters.

The Cloud Cover produced by Jet Engines is making the entire planet colder in winter even though the Carbon Dioxide gases produced by these same engines is also producing a Green House Effect or Global Warming. This means we're growing less food than we could for the planet and we're causing more and more people to die of starvation from it and at the same time requiring more electricity be produced to run our air conditioners in the summer and our heaters in the winter which is exacerbating the problem even more.

The DOT, the DOE and the EPA could be and should be set up to work with the Car Companies to produce ALL ELECTRIC VEHICLES and we should be using them in great numbers by now, but instead they merely rubber stamp what Detroit and all the other car companies want to produce. They could have been CHARGING a FEE for manufacturing Gas Powered Vehicles and using these fees to SUBSIDIZE the Car Companies conversion to All Electric Vehicles and Trains. Then, they could impose a fee for service on the High Speed Train riders and thus create their PROFITS.

With these profits, they contribute to the General Corporate coffers of the United States Government, instead of draining them and again we ALL get a DIVIDEND for being United States citizens and working our jobs in this new kind of economy where we're all pulling in the right direction. There are literally hundreds more ways in which the Division in charge of our transportation could make a profit. I have shown here only one of the most obvious ways to do this. They themselves could teach us many more, if they were given the chance. I would wager that many thousands of Dept of Transportation workers could show us the ways if they were incentivized to do so.

Instead, under our current system of LOSING MONEY every month, if they try to innovate, they are discouraged and even marginalized and demoted to a back office somewhere where they cannot be heard. The Dept of Health and Human Services. Now, there's a misnomer if I've ever seen one. When did this division in our Government ever make for better health care in this country? In fact, as we write this book, President Obama is holding a summit conference in Washington to try to pass his Health Care Reform bill that would have a price tag of ONE TRILLION DOLLARS.

They've already spent about TEN TRILLION of our tax dollars in the budget of the Dept of Health and Human Services. This agency has over 100,000 workers and yet they could not perform any health care reform with all that money we paid them? They have allowed so much WASTE, FRAUD AND ABUSE under this agency that under the current Obama Health Care Reform bill, one of the sections talks about NOT ALLOWING anyone who has DEFRAUDED MEDICARE to DO IT AGAIN.

YOU MEAN THEY DON'T DO THIS NOW? You currently allow Medicare fraud artists to GET YOU OVER AND OVER? Must be true, because the regulation today has to be in that 2,400 page Reform Bill. Why did we allow this agency to SPEND TEN TRILLION DOLLARS over the past fifty years if it was NOT to regulate our health care and shape it so that it would work and NOT REQUIRE another TRILLION to fix? How is that possible? Because the government does not have any incentive to MAKE a PROFIT, so they take the position this means they are supposed to LOSE MONEY, SO THEY DO THEIR BEST at this job of losing our money.

Hate to repeat myself over and over, but it has to SINK IN before most of us really SEE IT.

There is simply no other explanation. No one could have employed that many incompetent people? It's in the culture. The LOSE MONEY mentality in government is all-pervasive and controls the thinking process of everyone involved. If they started with the proposition that they had to MAKE A PROFIT, things would be far different.

So, the secret to the Government making a profit AS A WHOLE is simply to require that all of its corporate divisions – the AGENCIES - make a profit. It's really that simple. Some divisions will not be able to make a profit due to a Natural Disaster. FEMA for example could not be held to this general rule during a Hurricane such as Hurricane Katrina where they were forced to provide thousands of temporary housing units for people to live in. However, during periods of NO emergencies FEMA could be selling us all Preparedness Kits, bottles of water, dehydrated food, etc, so that we would all BE PREPARED for any natural disaster.

Now, let's try a tough one. Let's look at the DEPT. of the TREASURY. Basically, this is our Accounting Department for our national corporation. The Treasury prints our money, they look after the revenues by controlling the IRS. They count up all the beans and tell us how much money we made or lost, in any calendar year. HOW would we make this department a profit center?

If I solve this seemingly overwhelming business problem for you, then I hope you can see that any agency could be profitable once we put our minds to id. This is like asking the Accounting Dept of the company you work for to show a profit for its activities. It's never done. It's taught in most business management courses that Accounting will never bring you a profit because their only task is to COUNT THE BEANS it's NOT the MARKETING DEPT.

But actually, where the Treasury got themselves off their mission was when they went to the world and told them that the US DOLLAR would become the WORLD RESERVE CURRENCY. This rule they imposed on the world by guess who – NIXON – was the first step toward our eventual bankruptcy because it meant that the Untied States did not have to BALANCE the BOOKS ANY MORE. That's why NIXON wanted it.

What's the way out of this decades OLD PROBLEM? REVERSE the ENTIRE SITUATION. MAKE OUR COUNTRY HAVE TO BALANCE THE BOOKS AGAIN by INCORPORATION. If we don't do it THIS WAY, the world will force it on us in the form of AUSERITY MEASURES imposed by CHINA and JAPAN and RUSSIA. Let's continue to study how to throw the BUM ideas from the BUM PRESIDENTS OUT THE WINDOW and head towards a more intelligent form of management.

If the Dept of the US Treasury wanted to they could create many new ways of charging for their services and showing a profit. And, it has to do with the switch in our brains from taxing income and to taxing CONSUMPTION.

It also has to do with making the switch from our nation having to borrow money every year to operate to having to make a profit every year and the borrowing literally goes away. This is basically implied in the notion that we switch our financing from DEBT to EQUITY financing. The wealthiest parts of our society will object of course to the REVOLUTIONARY principle because they like to buy US TREASURY BONDS, because of their supposed SAFETY and they merely CLIP COUPONS to live.

They receive INTEREST PAYMENTS on the money they loan our government. By switching from Debt to Equity financing, which Incorporation would entail, these people are not likely to make the switch in their minds, but they would once the Government defaults on all their bonds, which they will be forced to do under our current weight of debt.

This MASSIVE DEBT the biggest in HISORY - can never be paid off and everyone who is buying US Debt right now, at the moment, really have their heads in the sand. They cannot see that right around the corner their total nest- egg will be gone and no one will ever replace it. Forget about the loss of interest payments. They will not even get their principle back.

There are not now nor ever will be enough government funds to cover these losses or any other funds anywhere else. By merely turning our thinking to another very viable way to finance a corporation, ISSUING STOCK, instead of debt instruments, we solve this problem in one stroke of the pen.

And, herein lies where the TREASURY, the BEAN COUNTERS, the MONEY PRINTERS and CONTROLLERS can show us a profit. First of all, they would have to cut back on the number of bean counters and trim their agency down by tens of thousands of workers. We simply cannot afford, nor do we need millions of people counting the debt, when there is no debt. They would be stealing their salaries under this system.

So, they must be either transferred or laid off. Now, with a much more manageable budget than what we have not, nearly 100 Billion per year to count our beans, and chopping it to a few million dollars to count our beans, then all the Treasury has to do is impose a very modest fee on the banks who the Treasury is sending all of our money to in order to be disbursed in loans to individuals and businesses. This is the heart of the economy.

All of the Treasuries Sub-Agencies such as the SEC, the agency that regulates stocks and bond trading on the stock exchanges, the FTC, the CFTC, the CFTC, the SIPC, the FIRC, FHA, FEA, ABC, etc. All regulatory authorities should EACH charge enough in fees to their respective industries that they are each able to report a profit to the Treasury.

In this way, the Treasury can actually regulate something and make a profit doing do. But all of this implies that these agencies all DO THEIR JOBS as well and that's where the bureaucrats will FIGHT US.

NOW, the IRS. Under our 'Pop Corporatism' plan, the IRS would be more involved with accounting procedures and keeping track of all the profits and HOW to PAY US the SHAREHOLDERS more equitably. NO MORE TAX FORMS, but instead, the IRS would be rewarding us with SHARES of stock as we became more and more productive to society. The IRS would evolve more into a LOTTERY type of agency, deciding where to hand out the WINNINGS, instead of how to make us THE BIGGEST LOSERS every year.

I see the IRS as being the best agency for being in charge of the entire system of PAYMENTS to citizens, instead of being the agency we all fear and hate. They would be used to make sure that all the agencies are making a profit and using these profits in the most beneficial ways to continue to stimulate and inspire us all to be better and better. The IRS would become the cheerleaders, our mentors, our partners in working towards complete financial independence. What better group of people to do this than the people who used to be in charge of collections, now in charge of our favorite disbursements, the dividends of working for a well-run, highly organized Corporate Government.

Under this set of ideas then, it is not unacceptable to think about changing the way the government earns its revenues. We should change our entire concept of our relationship with government so that we force them to pay us and not vice versa. With this in mind, it would seem to me that a personal Income Tax should be replaced by a . . . a Drum Roll Please – A USAGE FEE on PERSONAL CONSUMPTION and not on personal income.

When you really think about it, a tax is a penalty and society should strive to penalize the worst activities of our people, not the best. Making a living, supporting your family, getting and keeping a job, earning money, is not a bad thing for society, rather it's a GOOD THING, so why do we penalize our citizens for doing GOOD things?

We should penalize people and raise funds for our corporate government by penalizing people who do bad things and consuming things, taking resources from the Earth is one of the BAD THINGS that we do as humans. It's different when we make a conscious choice to consume only recyclable materials. It's different when we make a conscious choice as consumers to eat less meat because animals in large industrial farms are treated horribly before they are slaughtered. When we purchase fish or other foods that come from animals that are endangered from over-fishing as Tuna is today, this is a BAD THING for the planet and ourselves as a society because the more we deplete our planet of her resources, the sooner is the day of our own extinction.

Therefore, a CONSUMPTION tax is the best way for any government to raise funds so that it can guide society to eventually do the GOOD things, the LESS HARMFUL THINGS for the planet. The Government should be first and foremost a GOOD STEWARD of the Earth and a form of National Security second, only because, as logic would have it, if we destroy our planet, there's no reason to defend any portion of it, since without the right STEWARDSHIP, it would soon ALL be gone.

Make sense? It does make sense to me. In other words, there should be a higher tax on large gas-guzzling cars than smaller more efficient ones because large gas-guzzlers use up more oil that has to be sucked up out of the Earth, refined by large ugly chemical processing plants and then transported all over the planet where the ships leak this toxic poison into the ocean and into the air, killing forests and making our own breathing more and more difficult, creating climate change and catastrophic weather patterns that we are suffering today.

Making this type of vehicle more and more costly to the consumer is one way to discourage the manufacture and purchasing of this monster consumer item and so in this way, our government, now a wiser steward of our planet is making and enforcing the best policies to support our long term survival and the survival of our planet.

A consumption tax should be graduated according to the amount of damage that any product or service does to the Earth. For example, the tax on gas guzzler cars should be at least 5 to 10 times higher than the tax on a Toyota Prius. Everything that is purchased by the consumer is fair game to raise revenues for our new form of government, but a Toyota Prius that gets an average of 50 miles to the gallon and with better batteries just on the horizon will soon be getting more like 100 miles to the gallon is a much less harmful product to the Earth and therefore, a Consumption Tax of a few hundred dollars would be in order for a vehicle like this as opposed to a Consumption Tax of several THOUSAND DOLLARS for the Cadillac Escalade or the HumVee.

In this type of taxing environment, car manufacturers, in order to compete, would of necessity have to make smaller more fuel efficient cars to gain the lesser rates of taxation. So, the Consumption Tax, over the long term, helps in our over all survival as a society whereas an income tax does nothing for the planet or even less for the individual wage earner.

The Consumption Tax on things that are harmful to society on a degree that is significantly larger than the tax on things that are less harmful is the best way to raise funding for the government and help the consumption patterns improve our planet, rather than destroy it. Gradually, the avoidance of this tax will make for all products and services to be Earth friendly.

This could also mean that the revenues of the government will gradually decrease making the payment of dividends and the earning of a profit more and more difficult as time goes on. Therefore, there may need to be other forms of revenue for the government on top of the Consumption Tax. We already have sales taxes and estate taxes and other taxes on the books.

These should remain, but there could also be an energy tax and/or a travel tax placed on anyone renting a hotel or motel, and/or taxes for chopping down trees, destroying farmland for a strip mall and other taxes aimed at discouraging even more detrimental activities such as these. Flying in Jet Airliners should carry a special fee over and above the Consumption Tax because jet airliners create trails of exhaust that are now so prevalent that they block the sunshine and are now causing something called, GLOBAL DIMMING.

Global Dimming acts as a counter-balance to Global Warming and this is why we now have colder winters, tons of snow in the Winter even while we are having warmer and warmer summers. Wealthy people purchase their own private jet airplanes and this should have a luxury tax imposed on it, both the purchase of such a vehicle and the use of it, ON TOP of the Consumption Tax, Sales Tax and any other fees imposed on them because one or two people consuming thousands of gallons of jet fuel which puts tons of carbon dioxide into our atmosphere is OBSCENE, when they could be flying in commercial airliners, which are putting far fewer tons of exhaust into the air PER PERSON.

Just because someone can afford to trash our planet doesn't mean they have the right to do it. If we grant them the right to do it, it seems to me, we should make them PAY FOR THAT PRIVILEGE so that the rest of us can use the money to clean up their mess.

This graduated, more and more strict regulation of harmful activities by imposing greater and greater taxes on the worst offenders is a way to discourage harmful social behavior, reward good behavior, and help PAY TO CLEAN UP THE PLANET at the same time.

How does an income tax do any of these things? An income tax only serves to make people less incentivized to work hard because the harder you work, the more you pay the government in taxes under this system and that is unfavorable to a healthy economy. You want the hardest working, most creative, most industrious and innovative people to use all their talents to better improve the economy. The Consumption Tax is a method that matches the goals and missions of a government with a profit motive and a mission to save the Earth from human degradation that is now rampant.

This is a slightly different mission statement than most governments of the world whose sole purpose currently is to defend itself from neighboring nations or regions. If we raise the bar for the American form of government so that the entire world can see that we have changed dramatically from wanting to make war on other nations as well as on our own environment, then, there's hope for all Mankind. If we arrogantly continue on our present course of action where we build more and more powerful forms of self-annihilation, it's only a matter of time when we do kill off the human race. It's just that simple.

The laws of probability will eventually catch up to us and our selfish and profligate ways of spending our blood and treasure on mankind's most destructive endeavors, the War to End all Wars. That war is coming and there is not much the average person can do about it except trying to change the system that makes war possible in the first place.

If the goal of our government is to make a profit and pay its citizens enough in dividends to allow every citizen to live in happiness and prosperity, then Consumption Tax and not an Income Tax is the way to go. Most economists will argue that the American Economy is now based on the Consumer's spending and they would be correct, however, does it make sense for an entire economy, especially the economy of a world power to base its economy on your mother and mine going shopping every day at the mall?

Isn't this the kind of economy that killed the Roman Empire and the British Empire? I think the better question for economists is how to re-vamp our economy so that it is based on the manufacture and creation of goods and services that help to shape our planet in ways that will sustain our species for centuries and even eons into the future, and discourage the manufacture and creation of goods and services that destroy our planet and worsen our chances of survival as a species. The basic formula for this kind of federal revenue generation should be to have a sitting commission who meet on a regular basis and made up of environmentalists who have the expertise to assess just how much damage to the Earth that any product or service comprises.

The manufacture of a new car, as an example requires the mining of iron ore, the use of massive amounts of energy to smelt the ore and turn it into steel. The ore must be transported from the mines to the smelter and then the raw steel has to be hammered into body parts for the car, etc, etc. This type of process would have a Consumption tax that is far larger than the tax on a book, although a book has to be manufactured from paper that comes from trees, and so that environmental impact of a book would be greater than the impact of a piece of chewing gum and therefore the Consumption Tax for books is far greater than that for a piece of chewing gum.

The number of pages in a book like this one could be a factor, etc. etc. However, you should be reading this as an eBook, which is not as harmful to society as PRINT BOOKS that requires the chopping down of trees and therefore should have a consumptive fee attached to it HIGHER than an eBook. Everything must be put in a RELATIVE SCALE of how much harm something does to the planet in my opinion.

A product like a pair of shoes made from leather might have less of an impact than a pair of shoes made from rubber, therefore the tax for a pair of leather shoes would be less than the tax for a pair of rubber shoes. (Deriving leather from a steer, the animal may have already given its life for meat and so there could be less of an impact for leather than rubber. But, it could be the other way around.

I leave these kinds of decisions to the experts.) And so on and so forth until we have nearly every product or service in the economy tagged with an environmental sliding scale of impact and thus the tax each year is adjusted for industry improvements in this area and then the tax is assessed and updated accordingly. Most of these revenues would go into the profit motive of the Government, but some of it would go into the recycling of these materials to mitigate the damages done by them to our planet.

The need to impose much larger taxes on cars and trucks is so that we have the resources to recycle old cars and truck materials so that they go back into the Earth and ultimately having the least negative impact as is humanly possible. With this kind of planning and policy-making, this process would gradually lead to a planet where all cars and trucks were made of paper or a new type of plastic that is biodegradable in such a way that ZERO IMPACT would be made by these future vehicles.

THIS CAN BE DONE, if the will of the planet's governments are focused on this most important problem we face today. Clothing could eventually be produced from genetically engineered bacteria who produce a chemical that makes our artificial materials vanish into pure water and carbon within 2 months of being disposed of. Computers could eventually be made that used instead of batteries, solar power panels so sensitive that they even work at night under a lamp.

These things are all possible in our technological society, but they must be directed and formed as long-term policy by our political leaders. Greed must be controlled and discouraged in all the other ways we have outlined in this book and dividends for producing an economy that makes a profit must be paid to all shareholders in an equitable manner. Some people will say that this form of revenue generation will bankrupt the Federal Government, but actually I believe the opposite will happen.

I believe this form of taxation would increase revenues greatly. How? Think about it. Currently almost half of all citizens pay no income tax at all. There are 20 million illegal aliens who pay no income tax and about 40 million people who work in an all cash environment so that there is no way for the IRS to track them and they pay no income tax This makes for a terrific imbalance where people who are forced to pay their taxes do so grudgingly and think very begrudgingly of the element in society who gets away with non-payment and this is not healthy for any society.

IF this unfair system of Taxation is replaced with a consumptive tax, then everyone whenever they buy something pays their fair share of taxes, no forms to fill out, no sweating over horrible 1040's every April 15th, something that takes millions of man hours every year away from productive work we could all be doing for the economy. So, in this manner, we actually stimulate the economy by having more time to do the things that stimulate it instead of hamper it and frustrate us all. Those who consume the most would pay the most.

What is more fair than that? True the wealthiest segments of society would be able to buy more things, but they would be paying much more in taxes whenever they make a purchase and this is where revenues would increase. There would be no way to cheat the system. Every merchant who sells something already has to keep records, this would be a report they make at the end of the quarter and mail in their taxes they collected to that point. There would be no deductions. There would be no forms, no tax attorneys and no accountants who specialize in avoiding the income

Taxes for the wealthy, and this segment of society is freed up for more productive types of accounting. All of us, instantly would become more productive and more able to spend because there would be nothing withheld from our wages. Now, whenever we buy something, we'd pay Uncle Sam, but the bare necessities of life, food, most clothing items, a roof over your head would be exempt.

The IRS should be there to make sure that all merchants are withholding and depositing their Consumption Taxes properly and enforce the collection of same, just as the local state agencies do now for their Sales Taxes now found in most states. So, there is no added burden on merchants. True, there are a few more merchants added to the roles of collecting the Consumption Taxes, but they already do a fair bit of accounting and thus producing one more report and making one more payment is not going to kill any of them.

Current trade imbalances that favor China are that way because we consumers in the United States want to buy cheap shoes and T-Shirts, so the manufacturers have taken these jobs to China and other places where there is no regulation, no environmental safeguards and so you have areas in China that pollute the rest of the planet so much today that it's making breathing more and more difficult. The Chinese pollute more than any other country and they manufacture more junk for Americans to buy cheap and the planet is going to hell in a basket because this is the world's only economic model.

Make things cheaply and get more and more people to buy them. If you ruin the Earth, and that's OK? I hardly think that's very intelligent from the planet's supposed most intelligent creatures. Well, we're rapidly approaching the end game of this kind of careless and dangerous thinking. What we need now is a new kind of economist who can help us change our economy, and our economic model.

Taxation is a big part of any economic model because the taxing authorities can use graduated levels of tax to make industries thrive that are Earth friendly and discourage industries that destroy the planet and this currently is our only hope. What I'd like my readers to do now is make a list of all the harmful products and services they can think of and how much they'd be willing to pay in a fee to help discourage others from buying them. This should be an eye-opening experience.

Finally one more great example is the Space Program. As of the publishing of this book, NASA has turned over all major Space Exploration over to Private Companies. The Private companies will of course be held accountable to their investors to make a profit from their Space ventures. The government will presumably, after we get over the transition period COULD MAKE A PROFIT in partnership with these private corporations. People will be paying for trips into orbital hotels. Telecommunications companies will pay to have their satellites maintained in space. Isn't that the way it should be? Why not privatize all other Government agencies? This is the theme of this book. IF NASA can do it, so can every other government agency.

CHAPTER TEN – Pop Corporatism – The Ultimate IPO

The Enabling legislation for this great change is provided to us by the founding fathers of this great nation by allowing us the right to AMEND the Constitution any time we see it. Therefore, let's ensure that the next time this greatest of all documents is amended that it is amended for something powerful and beneficial to us all. AND NOT amended for something like the preservation of marriage and most Republicans are trying to push forward. The Amendment to the most sacred document ever conceived should be reserved for Real Change. The 28th AMENDMENT to the United States Constitution.

THE INCORPORATION AMENDMENT "Section 1.

The United States Government shall incorporate under the Common Laws of each of the several states and issue common stock (equity shares) to every American Citizen of voting age. Initial Stock valuations shall be made based upon the National Assets and Liabilities appertaining to the American Taxpayer at the time of issuance of stock. The value of such stock shall then fluctuate with the fortunes that such Equity in national assets may bring. Common Stock in the United States of America will then be traded on the various exchanges in any of the world stock markets.

Section 2. Congress shall have power to enforce this article by appropriate legislation." In order to ensure the continual monitoring and tweaking of the new Private Government Sector, the Voters must also be given the right to VOTE on ISSUES that are the most important to their well-being and security from time to time through the use of NATIONAL BALLOT MEASURES or National Initiatives and Referenda. And remember too that Congress is not going to be the usual bunch of suspects. Before, we ever get to this point, Congress - because of Google Super Vote - will be composed of people We The Ordinary voters have picked and have every aspect of kicking them out if they prove they don't have our interests at heart. Additionally, we have the power to control, reverse, amend or abolish any of their ideas as well.

Therefore the COMPANION AMENDMENT, the 29th, is such an amendment to protect the rights of the Citizenry to fine tune our economy and our political decisions at the will and the whim of the voters. I am currently considering a formula for VOTING THE SHARES that we as citizens will own in these National Referenda, but will save this for a future book on the topic, since the concepts are highly controversial and are what I call "Advanced Planning" for America 2.0, Inc. that I would like to save for later and after getting ideas from as many others as possible.

But, if you have been following the logic of this concept, we need to end up with enough shares in America 2.0 Inc. to be able to retire comfortably and I would hope that a value of at least ONE MILLION DOLLARS is attainable for every adult man and woman who attains retirement age. If a golden retirement, one in which all of one's needs are not provided for then what is the American Dream made of?

The other companion and key piece of this idea is that any nation needs its people be productive, to think more creatively, and to be innovative and even more hard-working and resourceful and be busy, instead of being distracted and corrupted by drugs or other vices that wastes a society's resources. Every contribution that fills one of these societal needs should be rewarded with additional stock throughout one's life.

AFTER the general populace is able to digest this basic concept first and foremost and wants to learn more. The basic problem that I am wresting with is that PEOPLE who do more for society should be given the opportunity to EARN more STOCK in AMERICA. In other words, someone who has worked diligently for their employer and stayed clear of any violations of the law, should earn more SHARES in America, than someone who is just entering the work force.

Then, if we allow shareholders to VOTE THEIR SHARES in these National Ballot Measures that I see as an ESSENTIAL PART to maintaining our Freedom, then, the older workers, the CEOS, the most successful entrepreneurs would have more say in the New

Democracy than younger people just starting out. I see this as a WIN/WIN/WIN proposition, but I am now taking discussion about this and other issues at my web site:

THE 29th AMENDMENT to the United States Constitution.

"Section 1. The right of citizens of the United States to vote on any issues brought before them on the Internet or that they deem the most urgent and of National importance through the process of a National Initiative and/or ballot measure which must pass by a two-thirds majority of voters. Voters get one vote per every share of stock in the United States of America that they own at the time of the ballot measure. Ballot measures that are on the official ballot will be placed there in order of their placement in several primary selection votes that shall put forth only the Top Ten vote getters in previous primary elections. Or they may end up on the National Ballot by acquiring the signatures ten percent of the total registered voters in any twenty-five of the states, or through a National Referendum placed on the ballot by a vote of three fourths of Congress. This amendment shall not be denied or abridged by the United States or by any state.

Section 2. The Congress shall have power to enforce this article by appropriate legislation." As mentioned above, this amendment on National Ballot Measures, may need upgrading to a way for The Shareholders in America 2.0, Inc. to vote their shares. I believe this is a higher form of Equity in that if someone has done more for society, they get more say in the direction and policy making of that society.

It's almost a TRIBAL CONCEPT that goes back thousands of years when we followed a strong and experience ELDER who had seen the ups and downs of struggling with a very harsh environment and the best leaders were those who used their experience in the world to keep their clan away from danger. These clans who were successful, in true Darwinian Style would survive and evolution would continue to where we are today. I know, however, that there will be those who resist this kind of concentration of power to those who have contributed the most and the young people of this country may see it quite differently. After, all, it has been the elder folks of this nation that have led us INTO DANGER and not AWAY from it.

They may have a point. So, this part of my theory is open for debate and probably will remain that way for quite some time until time and distance can be achieved from our present calamity. I firmly believe that through the use of this greatest corporate entity in history, the United States of America Incorporated would finally be able to compete on the global economic stage. Other nations, after all, do not enjoy our tradition of Democracy and Liberty, our Freedoms of Speech, Freedom of the Press, the rights that allow for this type of debate to even exist, and therefore, it will be a number of generations before more primal economies will be able to find themselves in the same ball park, let alone on an even playing field with such a FORCEFUL ECONOMIC ENGINE as this.

Bear in mind also – because I know this subject will be controversial for years, perhaps decades, before it is adopted - Just because this kind of thing has never been done before, does not mean that the concept holds no merit. Many will call this RADICAL and REVOLUTIONARY, and indeed it may be, but it should be remembered that this nation, the greatest experiment in democracy in history was begun on just such a RADICAL AND REVOLUTIONARY IDEA; that . . .

"All men are created equal, that they are endowed by their Creator with certain unalienable Rights, that among these are Life, Liberty and the pursuit of Happiness. — That to secure these rights, Governments are instituted among Men, deriving their just powers from the consent of the governed, — That whenever any Form of Government becomes destructive of these ends, it is the Right of the People to alter or to abolish it, and to institute new Government, laying its foundation on such principles and organizing its powers in such form, as to them shall seem most likely to effect their Safety and Happiness."

The basic contract between the people and our present form of Government, what we must now call America version 1.0, (unincorporated) was laid on the principle that We The People are the very be-all and end-all for forming a government in the first place and that We The People are therefore it's TRUE OWNERS.

The only notion then, that Thomas Jefferson left out of this, historic Declaration of Independence of 1776 was that we should be actually be given stock to authenticate this ownership to strengthen the basic contract. I believe that if Tom Jefferson, and the rest of the Founding Fathers had experienced personally the advantages of modern Stock Ownership of corporations, he would have done so.

But, in 1776, stock ownership was strictly a tool in which the British Empire ruled the world, hardly a concept that would have been popular in the 1776 American colonies, in a real revolt away from British domination.

IN CONCLUSION: A discussion of the Amendment process Although highly innovative and outside the norm, the Incorporation of the United States of America is NOT impossible. The US Constitution has been amended 27 times to date. The most important amendments to our Constitution are the 9th and 10th Amendments passed as what is known as the Bill of Rights.

The First Amendment grants us the now famous rights to free speech, freedom of the press, freedom of religion, the right to PETITION our Government for a better and improved form of government - the very foundation of democracy. And, of course we now take all of these freedoms for granted. But the most important amendments, the 9th and 10th, are the ones that we should study the most.

Amendment 9 states: The enumeration in the Constitution, of certain rights, shall not be construed to deny or disparage others retained by the people. And Amendment 10 states: The powers not delegated to the United States by the Constitution, nor prohibited by it to the States, are reserved to the States respectively, or to the people.

In other words, what the founding fathers are saying: "If the American people of the future are desirous of any further rights or basic changes to these rights, those rights are hereby granted." Then, they go on to specify how we go about gaining those additional rights and it is through the Amendment Process. The Constitution, under this granted process has been amended 27 times so far.

That's about one every ten years on average. Every school child knows that it was the 13th Amendment to our Constitution in 1865, pushed through by President Lincoln, that ended once and for all the atrocity of slavery in this country. Interestingly, Slavery had been legal for the first one hundred years of our history. And, it would take another century for the rights of former slaves to become enforced in the Southern half of our country. In 1913 the Constitution was again amended to allow the federal government to tax our incomes.

The 28th and 29th Amendment above are my own expressions of what should come next. One could even argue, what good is there in any of the previous two hundred years of amendments unless we are all freed, not just the black slaves imported from Africa to grow our crops? When do we all gain our freedom from involuntary servitude. It certainly was not the intention of the founding fathers to have us living like this, just as it was not the intent of the founding fathers that we be prohibited from drinking beer and wine.

Somehow, over time, through criminal mismanagement and malfeasance in office, unprecedented bungling and outright fraud and theft of our assets and national pride, we now work for the banks and the foreign investors who own our nation, lock stock and barrel. In a way, the AmBush cronies on Wall Street who took this greed to the ultimate climax may have done us all a favor by exposing the corrupt system of voodoo economics for all of us to see quite plainly.

It should be clear to even the most casual observer of United States political history that through the last two centuries of our evolution of democracy, the basic trend that is striking is the trend toward more and more individual freedom. In the very first amendment, we allow for the freedoms that we take so much for granted of speech, press, religion, etc. In the next set of amendments, we make slavery illegal and allow women the right to vote take away and then give back the right to make and consume alcoholic beverages.

Over the grand sweep of our history we have altered our basic social and political contract so that the voting rights are more clear and open to more and more people and more classes of people. We make it easier for people to vote and we even specify how fast Congress can raise their own salaries. The only amendment that goes against the grain of more and more freedom is the 13th Amendment that allowed our federal government to tax our incomes. Perhaps it's time to rectify this problem along with the glaring problem of our NOT being INCORPORATED.

Contrary to what Supreme Court Justice Antonin Scalea has stated publicly our Constitution is NOT DEAD, as Scalea believes. It is a living document that has changed through the centuries and will change dozens more times. Appointed by Ronald Reagan, Scalea shows his incompetence for the job by stating publicly that our Constitution, something he is sworn to defend, is a dead document. If it ever dies, we're in a whole hell of a mess.

The next amendment to our Constitution should not be a small and petty one, for example the one that Republicans are currently pushing the 'The Defense of Marriage Amendment. No, that is social engineering that is not the place for the Constitutional issues. This type of thing is a matter of conscience and something the states already have the power to do or not do. So, conservatives are using Red-Herring issues like this one to distract us from REAL CHANGES that are so sorely needed. They know we could think BIG as I'm doing here, but they will never agree to BIG CHANGES because that would dilute their power.

Instead of taxing us and taking from us to pay their operational expenses, it should and it can become the norm to PAY US – the SHAREHOLDERS out of our own national profits. So, the 28th and 29th Amendments should be followed up in the same sweep of time with the 30th Amendment that repeals the thirteenth, making Income Taxes illegal and perhaps replacing it with a Consumption Tax as we have discussed.

It's time to make these sweeping changes so that laws that we must all live by, the policies that can change the world for good or evil are no longer made my a select few, by committees, smoke-filled rooms, and the greedy and incompetent and the Two-Party System. This is the next step in the evolution of democracy.

In the founding years of this great nation, they could not grant freedom to everyone, or voting rights to both males and females. They couldn't allow everyone to vote and they certainly forced us to vote for a Representative who is then sent to Washington D.C. to vote in our best interests.

It is clear to most of us today that this antiquated system is no longer functioning in our modern technological world. We no longer tolerate slavery or the prejudice against women or any other minority. We can no longer afford to wait for modern problems to be solved by the horse-and-buggy mentality of a day gone by. We no longer have the time to wait for a Congress that once needed to be sent to a far away place to cast their votes. Today, politicians don't need to collect themselves into a single building to vote.

Think about what a waste of jet fuel that is. More importantly consider what a terribly small and insufficient brain trust we have in only a few hundred white men in business suits, lawyers at that.

We can vote over the Internet and from the comfort of our own homes at any time we want to do so and we can VOTE DIRECTLY on the ISSUES, not for some Party Member who has been appointed and anointed by the Two-Party system to vote for us. We're old enough as a nation and mature enough as a nation to vote for ourselves. In this way, the special interests, the wealthy folks, the 1%, the lobbyists, the vast and powerful corporations would have a much tougher time buying our votes.

OH, they will try. But it will be such a daunting task, that only a few national ballot measures will be influenced by them. No system will be perfect and they will find ways to corrupt even the hundreds of millions of us who would be voting in a Real Democracy. They will be successful more than I care to imagine. But at least, we will have more of a chance to get the right concepts established. Over time, the vast majority of national ballot measures will succeed on their own merits, either up or down.

Therefore, we must be finally given this last right of a real democracy in the form of National Ballot Measures because AS SHAREHOLDERS we have the right to vote in our own best interests and negate some of the idiotic and counter-productive things that our MANAGEMENT does to us. This is not only desirable, it is mandatory now. It is required if our future is to be secured. The point of this ending chapter is to point out to nay-sayers that it is NOT that difficult to amend the US Constitution as long as there is a good reason to do it and that this condition of reason and logic has been found to be true some 27 times already in our history.

No - Antonin Scalea, our Constitution is still very much alive and waiting patiently for us to breathe even more life into her now. And, Mr. Scalea, I tremble to think about how many decisions that effect so many lives have been made or influenced by you, someone who believes our Constitution to be DEAD. You owe it to your country to resign. Or, perhaps we can find a way to IMPEACH YOU. Your decisions, all of them, are suspect after you make a treasonous and deceitful statement like that. I wonder what your agenda has been all these years. Has it been to bring this country to its knees politically and economically? If so, you've done a good job.

Making a few more where the reasons are even greater than ever before to do them makes the most sense, at least to this writer. It seems almost ridiculous to think that women had to WAIT to gain the right to vote until 1920, almost two hundred years after the founding of this country, or that African Americans had to wait almost a century to gain equal status under the law and be freed from Slavery.

It almost makes you sick to think about it and how the great founding words were NOT meant for everyone. How did the founding fathers miss so much about Freedom in their first iteration of our country's basic document? It seems ridiculous to us today that anyone could be owned by another person as they would own a piece of furniture or a television set, yet this was also missed by our founding fathers.

They have ONE REDEEMING THOUGHT that MAKES IT ALL BETTER.

Thanks be to GOD that they did not miss the fact that they knew they were leaving a lot of things up to the imagination and that this imagination would have to come from future generations and so they gave us the right to AMEND or change or adapt our basic fundamental relationship to our management in ways that we can imagine today and of which we may imagine even more in the future.

This is the greatest and most saving feature of our government and it's time we took advantage of it. If we do not, it is becoming clearer and clearer to more and more of us that we will soon fail in the world political stage and other nations will rise to fill in our vacuum.

From there on, it would be very tough sledding for Americans if we allow other forms of government to prevail over us and like the tide, this is inevitable and is rising even now. So, the historical precedent, the legal logic is there in place right now to do this. The only reason not to do this is one of inertia and lack of momentum in this direction illustrated by the fact that we've not yet done it.

But, the fact that we've yet to do this, doesn't mean it cannot or must not be done. The Reasons NOT to do something as opposed to the Reasons TO DO something. Benjamin Franklin is famous for many things, but he is also famous for creating the best way for somebody to make a decision. On a piece of paper he draws a line down the middle making two columns.

On one column, he writes, 'Reasons To Do' and in the other column he writes: 'Reasons NOT to do' a thing, whatever it is we're deciding. Then, in the To Do Column he writes every reason to do this thing and in the Not to do column, he writes every reason not to do this thing. Then, he counts them up and makes his decision based on which column has the most reasons.

In this book, I have listed most of the Reasons TO DO this thing and I leave it up to others to list the reasons NOT to do this thing, because honestly, I personally can't see any good reasons not to. Some of my readers will have reasons in their minds NOT to do this thing, to Incorporate the United States of America into America 2.0 Inc. and I have already read a few arguments against it at my Quora Account. If you want to voice your opinion please go to – http://Quora.com/Michael-Mathiesen and get into the discussion.

Most of the arguments I have heard AGAINST doing this were from people who just gave me their knee-jerk reaction. It's like if I said to you. Coca Cola should taste more like Ollalieberries. Well, almost everyone would want to keep the taste of a bottle of cold refreshing Coke the same. And, they would not know what Ollalieberries tasted like or if they did, how it would blend in with their old familiar taste. So, they might be against it.

This kind of REVOLUTIONARY IDEA, something that is on the CUTTING EDGE of consciousness, has to be incubated in one's mind. You have to go over the pro's and cons. You have to think about the present form of our government and compare something this new and different to the one we have, a system in which we have come to a complete wrenching halt in reason and logic and in evolution. In fact, one could easily make the case that America is now going BACKWARDS under the mis-management and ineffectual and worthless ideas of the last several decades, such as invading Viet Nam, invading Iraq and spending TRILLIONS of dollars to kill the wrong perpetrator of 9/11, a scapegoat made up by the AmBush administration. I call him that because not only did he lead our soldiers into an AmBUSH in Iraq, but after that incredible evil, he AmBushed the entire global economy in the last few months of his tyranny by letting his cronies on Wall Street ROB US ALL BLINE, not only US, but the rest of the world.

This mismanagement is simply not good for the long haul, my dear readers. Our current lack of a real system of management of our economy is leading us all into financial chaos. The rule of the 1% over the rest of us, the 99% is anathema and counter to all things we call Democracy.

And, think about this for a minute. Why do we allow Initial Public Offerings of groups like FaceBook, something so meager, so tiny to the health and welfare of the rest of us, when the health, welfare and happiness of the rest of us could stand the same process. After all, facebook is an internet concoction where people can tell their friends what they're doing minute by minute. How many of us really need to know what our friends are doing minute by minute? How does that get us through our every day survival?

Why not a place not on the Internet, but in the REAL WORLD where we can tell each other what we're THINKING about our country, about our economy, about our Political WILL? Which Public Offering of stock makes more sense to you?

Why not have an Initial Public Offering for something that would be truly beneficial not only to the other 99% of all Americans, but if and when this model is emulated by other nations, would impact so powerfully the rest of the world, putting us all on the next great plateau of civilization? Why not? Can you think of any reasons why NOT to do this and do it NOW, before it's too late.

Yes, the Earth could be FLAT, but Christopher Columbus sailed his three ships off the Flat Earth and proved that it was round and in the process, discovered America, at least for the Europeans. It had already been discovered by the Native Americans, of course.

Just as the establishment thinking said that the 'Earth is Flat' there will be some who say it's crazy to incorporate this government. Some will call it Socialism. But, what we have now is a hybrid Socialist State and Capitalist state without the REAL benefits of either because of the huge weight on our shoulders of the Bureaucracy, constantly making up silly and useless rules. Great job security, making up silly and useless rules, but it's hardly what makes a country or an economy BOOM.

So, if you want to side with the Flat-Earthers, come up with reasons why we should not or cannot make this kind of

Revolutionary Change. But, if you want to side with the best logic and reason of the Future, come up with ways you can help.

Someday, there will be an Initial Public Offering of Stock in the United States of America, v 2.0, Inc. I'm very confident of that. I just don't know, nor do I expect that it will happen in my lifetime or even the lifetimes of most of my readers. That it could happen in the lifetime of my children, gives me great solace. I hope someday they'll understand why I spent countless hours putting my dreams down in a form that might spread to others.

CHAPTER ELEVEN: The First Internet Constitutional Convention

All of the words of this book and all other political diatribes are useless until mixed with some real live action on the part of the people. I'm fully aware that some of my ideas, if not all, will be totally wasted on us all until and unless there's some method put forward for making these kinds of changes become reality.

There is only one way to do this. We must now call everyone to a Constitutional Convention. I call it the first Internet Constitutional Convention because I believe we could hold such an event over the Internet and invite literally millions of concerned America citizens to attend.

The details of holding such a political convention, I leave to others. I believe I have done my part is making the public appeal and providing all Americans with plenty of things to discuss at such an historic event.

I do know from my extensive use in making my living over the Internet for these last couple decades that the technology of today's Internet does include enough in the way of online meeting and conferencing tools and sharing tools that would allow for the rapid publication of the ideas expressed at such an online convention.

At the very least, we need a few good programmers to create a safe and secure database so that each and every American with a potential solution to a problem be allowed to put that solution or invention of theirs onto a comment form of some kind, whereupon all the rest of us could vote it up or down, pushing the best ideas to the top of the heap and the worst ideas to the bottom, with some of them being ignored, and others being given gradually more and more consideration.

We would then take the best ideas that make it to the top of the process and put them to a brainstorming session where we would debate each word and phrase and break down all possible outcomes that each carefully selected and filtered proposal might have on society. The, after a set period of days, all debate and alteration is ceased and a final vote put forth to the convention attendees. Eventually, by the time that the convention closes, we would have an agreed upon action for the country to adopt and history would be made as the next version of The United States of America is born.

If this process seems impossible or alien to you, just remember that this was the exact process that was shaped by the founding fathers in the first Constitutional Convention of 1789 and the outcome of that activity was the United States Constitution, with all of its flaws intact. At the birth of this country, it is fair to point out, slavery was legal because most of the founding fathers were slave-owners and they were not about to make their own activities illegal. They would be long gone when slavery was finally abolished in 1865 under President Abraham Lincoln.

Therefore, if history is our guide, we will emerge this time with another flawed Constitution this time, but over time it will be amended, just like the first version of America has been amended some twenty-seven times and at some point in time, it will serve the American people more fairly and equitably than ever before and this time perhaps for centuries more.

We can already use the existing technology supplied to us by Google especially Google SuperVote plus Facebook, Google Plus, Twitter, LinkedIn, Youtube, Quora, Tumblr, Pinterest etc. for the rapid dissemination of knowledge. Therefore, I have no doubts that new iterations of this kind of social networking can be put to higher and better use for the overall political and economic survival of this country. The improvements that we can put into place will be so much more astounding than what I have outlined here that it cannot be understated just how much change, or how many changes we will soon be allowed to make.

We only need he wisdom and experience of using such a system to allow us to prevent too much and too rapid a change where all citizens, regardless of their status in life can comprehend and adapt to. Changes must be incremental at best and in the beginning, more thought out and planned and analyzed than any decisions that have been made in the past because if we push the wrong buttons in the early stages of America 2.0, our enemies will use that to try to crush our revolution. Therefore, all thoughts, all potential solutions to the real problems facing us every day must go through the most exhausting of tests and trials and even hurdles.

To give this some real impetus in your minds, harken back to the decision made by a very few men in power at the time, George W. Bush and his advisors in the White House who conspired to sell us the fake story that Iraq possessed the famous "WMD" or Weapons of Mass Destruction" and that one day soon, we might even see a nuclear mushroom cloud bursting into the skies of an American city. Nothing could have been further from the truth, but because of this lie, the people of this country were forced to spend a whopping TWO TRILLION DOLLARS and the price tag is still growing due to the ongoing Veterans Benefits of this involvement, more than 10,000 American soldiers were killed, hundreds of thousands of innocent Iraqis were slaughtered by American bombs, men, women and children, besmirching the great name of this country and one man, Saddam Hussein was forced from power over his own people.

I am willing to stake my life on the fact that if this proposal were put to the American people by President Bush and he stated publicly that he would abide by the decision of the American voters on this subject, and if we had known of the costs of this war, not a single thinking American would have voted 'YES' to go ahead and invade Iraq under such penalties to our own welfare and with so little to gain.

At the present time, it appears that nothing has been learned by the succeeding administration since it is clear as of the time of this writing that President Obama is highly agitated by the actions of a similar brutal ruler in the region and now he is hard at work trying to convince Congress to begin the same kind of military operation in Syria. They appeal to us under the banner of 'MORAL INDIGNATION'. But, are they ignoring the moral indignation of millions of Americans who are out of work and suffering, many millions of us still homeless after the collapse of 2008? Are they trying to cause another larger collapse by ignoring their more pressing responsibilities at home?

Therefore, it is blatantly obvious to me and I think the rest of my countrymen that a new form of democracy needs to replace this old worn-out Republican form of government where our leaders are able to completely ignore their own sworn responsibilities to serve the interests of their own country FIRST, SECOND and THIRD and the interests of other countries much further down the line.

IF the bombing of this new supposed threat to our security, Syria a country who can't even defend themselves against their own people is so important to someone in the administration, why in the name of all that's holy won't the President put this to the PEOPLE themselves? He has said publicly that he doesn't even need the permission of Congress, yet my reading of our Constitution says he does. Since, he was a professor of Constitutional Law in Chicago before he ran for President, I suppose he knows something the rest of us don't.

It is clear from all other major decisions of this nature that Presidents have continually gotten our country into hot water and there is only one President in my lifetime who could actually balance the budget - Bill Clinton. Sadly there is only one of those.

But what if we forced them to balance the budget every year or be punished by having their pay withheld, put into an escrow account until such time as the budget is in balance?

With National Ballot Measures, this potential solution amongst countless others could be put forth and the people allowed to decide them. A Congress would never allow itself to be controlled in such a way by their own people, and therefore, don't expect and completely common sense and useful laws like this to be passed by Congress. That will never happen because the only thing they worship is money. This has been proven over and over again.

One of my themes throughout this book is that we must incorporate the entire Government because under our present NON-PROFIT organization, where our leaders have the mission of wasting as much money as is humanly possible, something different, perhaps even the opposite of what is so horribly broken must be tried.

Even though this form of government where the corporate leaders are charged with making profit from all of their activities, the people have a foundation for a kind of prosperity never before achieved in human history. One thing I've learned from my business career is that when you give people incentives to work hard and make money - they do precisely that.

If it proves to be impossible to include all of my suggestions in the version of America 2.0, I don't care. If only we take control of our government through National Ballot Measures, my life's dream of a real democracy on this planet once again is fulfilled.

We must remember that they had a real democracy during the Golden Age of Greece over 2,000 years ago. Since that time, only half-baked versions of the democratic system of governance have been adopted anywhere on the planet. The main argument that we could put against adopting a real democracy that holds any water at all is that we simply did not have the technology to take the votes of all the voters in a reasonable amount of time, thus we sent representatives to one building in Washington where they could gather together and hold votes that could be tallied quickly.

Today, however, we can tally votes of the entire American electorate in less time than it takes them to tally the entire Congress and with far better assurance that our votes will not be compromised by the outrageous and constant bribery that we see happening every day in the halls of Congress.

If there be anyone who doubts the laws passed under the rule of bribery, just take a look at all the recent and most important bills that are over ONE THOUSAND PAGES LONG. The Congress men and women aren't even given enough time to read the very bills they are required to vote on and pass or fail. Bills this long can only be that way because of all the special interests, the lobbyists inserting their favorite clauses, paragraphs and even entire chapters in the bills.

There is no reason for any proposed law to be more than a few paragraphs so that anyone can understand them. Even if we wanted to reform our complex tax laws, that could be done in just a few paragraphs if we chose to do so.

If, for example, there was a proposal on the ballot to abolish the entire US Tax Law, that could be stated in one sentence. AND, the replacement revenues could be proposed in the second sentence.

"The US Tax Regulations on personal income are hereby repealed in their entirety. In order to replace revenues required to run our government, all personal incomes above $50,000 per year shall be taxed at 10% and the first $50,000 being exempt from any tax. All income above $100,000 Per year shall be taxed at 20% and all personal income above $200,000 per year shall be taxed at 30% whereupon it is not increased until income exceeds one million dollars per year wherein all income above one million dollars shall be taxed at 50%."

The only reason we do NOT get proposals like this passed into law on a daily basis is because the lobbyists who represent the TAX ATTORNEYS and TAX ACCOUNTANTS who make their living under our current over-complicated set of rules would BRIBE CONGRESS to not even consider such a proposal as the one I've outlined above.

However do you have any doubt the majority of American voters would in fact pass such a proposal if it were placed on the ballot?

No more complicated tax forms that we struggle to fill out every year. No more having to find software to prepare out tax returns for us. Everyone would be able to fill in their returns in an average of five minutes. You take your income and look at the tax and send it in or get a refund depending on how much you chose to have withheld. That simple. No more tax attorneys, no more CPA's billing us hundreds of dollars per hour just to determine how much we owe every year.

One more example of how easy it would be to run our country using the wonderful technology of the Internet.

WE DO NOT NEED CONGRESS to do our bidding any more!

HERE'S ONE MORE EXCELLENT EXAMPLE OF HOW TO USE GOOGLE SUPERVOTE and NATIONAL REFERENDA

* * * National Ballot Measure Number XXXX * * *

"The 'Patriot Act' is hereby repealed in its entirety."

That's how easy it would be once we reorganize our government in favor of National Ballot Measures. Would you vote for such a law? If you thought about the recent abuses of our government under the rules of the Patriot Act, which suspended key elements of our sacred Constitution and that it is just another act away for them to completely wipe out all our freedoms, then I hope that you would vote to repeal such an ill-advised law put into effect under the treasonous rule of the George W. Ambush administration.

AND, this proposal as written above is all that is necessary to take back our full freedoms of due process under our Constitution.

There is not a word more that would be required. Leave this kind of thing up to CONGRESS and they would make it ten thousand pages long so that in the end no one would know if the Patriot Act is repealed or not or even if we had made the situation worse.

Remember, everything that I have shown in this book can be put to the test over the Internet in its present form. In a few years, we could also improve the Internet so that there can never be any hacking or skull-duggery of that kind. We could also make it easier for everyone to have access to the Internet and even make it universal, a requirement for the telephone companies and cable companies to deliver to every customer for free if we have to.

There are no impediments to our using the Internet in the next political Revolution. There are no limitations to what we could achieve. We would have our country firmly in the control of those who the government is sworn to serve. The last several decades have proven that a Representative form of democracy no longer serves the people because over time, they have allowed forces that are unconstitutional - essentially the lobbyists - to take control of our system. Therefore, our present system is no longer viable. It cannot be reformed under its present system without a complete and total revolution as we have described above because the illegal and immoral system of bribery that is now extant simply would never allow such reforms since it would put them out of power.

Is there any doubt that We The People desperately need America to be altered in this revolutionary and modern way. The rest of the world is patiently waiting for the leader of the free world to redefine what we mean by freedom. If we do not empower the people of America to become truly free, then there is no reason why we should be called the leader any more. New players will take our place.

I make one last appeal to every reader of this book to do their utmost to spread the word of these ideas. The mainstream media has blocked this information reaching the masses for decades. I have written countless letters to the Editors. I have reached out to all politicians I could to appeal to their common decency to at least debate the idea of using National Ballot Measures, but all to no avail.

I can tell you that there is a vast conspiracy to censor this information and prevent the American people from learning the truth. We will only change this government by the concerted actions of millions of us banding together and demanding these changes at every opportunity.

Contact your local TV and radio stations and keep pestering them until they do a news story about us or your activities in the local community. Create your own strategies, rattle the cages a bit, and then get these activities some media coverage, large or small. Eventually the Flat-Earthers will have to concede. When the media comes around, it will be inevitable. Resistance is futile..

Mohatma Gandhi said: "First they ignore you. Then, they laugh at you. Then, they fight you. Then you win." We're in the 'ignore us' phase so far. With a little effort on your part, we'll soon get the the 'Laugh at us" stage. Then, the rest is pre-destined.

Let's all start rowing in the same direction. Let's incorporate this government and allow everyone all around the world to take stock in America 2.0, Inc, Let us all prosper in this new world order of prosperity and common equity. I invite and eagerly await your participation and look forward to same.

I also invite criticism, discussion and debate at my web site. And Finally I want to add this thought. The US Supreme Court recently decided in the 'Citizens United' Case that "Corporations are People".

This decision cannot be over-ruled or overturned by any body in this country. Since the Supreme Court is, other than God, the ultimate authority on all things political, this ruling has become a fact of Nature. It's the same thing as a corporation being born to a human woman.

There is no difference in the way that a human being is now to be treated under the law as compared to any legal corporation in good standing. And, so since a corporation is now a person, by the same logic a government, the sum and substance of all humans who live in its jurisdiction can become a master corporation, a holding company if you will, whose mission it is to serve and protect all human citizens living under it's rule.

There only needs to be now, a meeting of the minds, the forming parties, the Corporate Charter and bylaws and a Board of Directors. Those are the basic elements of a corporate entity. I hope that this book provides a meeting of the minds, or at the very least a place to begin the meeting.

I propose that everyone who has digested this material carefully and thoughtfully may become part of the forming parties, that the information in this book form the basis of the Corporate Charter, its mission and its bylaws.

And, the last step would be the actual wording of the amendments to the US Constitution that enacts this concept into law.

This will be a long arduous process because history teaches us that nothing this revolutionary and evolutionary will not come about without a great deal of controversy and adversity. Please also support our Web Site so that you can remain steadfast in the pursuit of the greatest change to the political system ever conceived.

Share the book, the web sites and this information with everyone you know as freely as it has been given and support the cause by purchasing one or more of my other books. All future generations of Americans may depend on your support today. www.America2inc.com

If, after reading this book – YOU DO NOTHING, then you are accepting the old worn-out and moribund Politics of the PAST and you don't mind the direction in which we're headed, the Road to Ruin.

IF you love your country and want to see some REAL CHANGE, then you will JOIN US to help start making the REAL CHANGE that we deserve as a people. If you are a Republican, we want you. If you are a Democrat, we want you and need you. If you are an Independent, we need you. If you are a Tea Partier, we need you. If you are a Libertarian, Green Party, Communist, Socialist, or any other Party, we need you to DROP ALL your current dogma or bend it to fit this great cause, the only way into the future where all ideas have a chance to thrive - and JOIN US.

START TELLING THE WORLD. We must all unite and work together for a CONSTITUTIONAL AMENDMENT to the United States Constitution that favors the INCORPORATION of the UNITED STATES GOVERNMENT for the sole purpose of forcing sound business principles on our leaders, not the least of which is making a profit and paying dividends to each and every American Citizen in return for our blood, sweat and tears. Is this not an idea whose time has come? I leave the answer up to you my readers.

But the path to all of this change is the one provided to us by Google, so if you want to help, all you have to do is send your friends to the website where they can purchase this book. By making this a best-seller, along with other strategies that you will start to read about, we can force Google to expand this amazing technology into a DEMONSTRATION SYSTEM for changing this country that eventually will become so popular that the people will DEMAND that it be put into place as the OFFICIAL way that we do our business as a Federal Government by giving ordinary people, the RIGHT TO VOTE, but voting not for Tweedle-Dee or Tweedle-Dumb but for something that is the opposite of dumb and is extremely advanced, and always right on target, voting for ideas that are the best ideas that the Wisdom of the Crowd is able to produce, faster, cheaper and better than any ideas coming out of the 'Puny and Under-Sized National Brain Trust' that is possessed by the Congress and President of the United States.

And, finally we've all seen the benefits of how when a new company is listed on the major Stock Exchanges, how instantly thousands of millionaires and sometimes even billionaires are created out of thin air. This is because a small group of entrepreneurs have created a product that benefits society in some small way, but in a large enough way that millions of people start to use their product. This makes them enough money and gains this group enough attention so that they gain access to the stock markets of the world.

What did they do to become instantly so wealthy? First, they produced a great product. Next, they formed a corporation to own that product. Next, they issued THEMSELVES, the founders of that company and some of their key employees millions of shares of STOCK in that corporation.

Then, they go public. In going public, they make their corporation open to anyone who has the money to buy some of these shares. If all goes well, the demand for their stock far exceeds the number of shares they have produced in that company, thus forcing the value of each share to skyrocket. This is when, these founding fathers and mothers of this corporation become totally financially independent and will have enough money to last the rest of their lives and even have plenty left over to hand down to their descendants.

As John Lennon might say - Imagine - if this same process were made available to EVERYONE who is a citizen of this great country. Instead of one product that has to catch on, we have millions of them. Instead of just a few founding fathers and mothers, we have every citizen to share our success with. Instead of being controlled by just a few wealthy people at the top of the heap, we control everything by VOTING OUR SHARES.

In the END, we all become wealthy and we do this by controlling our own destiny as a nation, One Nation finally and truly Under God! And one nation finally and truly 'OF THE PEOPLE, BY THE PEOPLE and FOR THE PEOPLE'.

# # #

ABOUT THE AUTHOR

Michael Mathiesen is a Science and Science Fiction Author living in beautiful Santa Cruz, California. Try one of his other books found below. Mathiesen became interested in real democracy in America when he was asked by President Nixon to join him and participate in the horror known as Viet Nam. It was this most perplexing moment in his life that made him realize there had to be a better way to conduct the affairs of what he, and many millions of other people all over the world considered to be the greatest country of all time. This book is a product of that life-long quest to make this country honor the promise of Real Democracy.

"Everyone I knew, millions of Americans, were protesting against this war. Yet, one man, Lyndon Johnson and then his successor Richard Nixon defied the will of the vast majority of American people and decided to have his little war despite public opinion, citing 'The Silent Majority'. According to Nixon, most people supported him by their silence. Until the invention of the Internet, we had no voice, so they could consider us a 'Silent Majority' and much of the evil in this world is perpetrated even today under this banner.

With Google Super-Vote and the rest of the Internet's wonderful technology the MAJORITY need not, nor can be silent any longer.

Discover Other books by this Author: http://MichaelMathiesen.com

STOP THE GOVERNMENT SPYING ON YOU - AND HELP OTHERS STOP the GOVERNMENT SPYING - http://CyberWealth7.com/Money

This software PREVENTS anyone from snooping on your computer while you're ONLINE - NOT EVEN THE NSA can break this Encryption Software - Help Get ALL AMERICANS PROTECTED from their own government. Make Money too!

For current news on these events and more ways that you can help save the world - Email me

MarketingCircles@gmail.com

<<<<< Help Support the Author >>>>>
<<<<< GoGoMLM.com >>>>>

Join My Online Business and Make Money From Home

If you liked this book. You're sure to enjoy my new Science Fiction Thriller -

Immortality: A True Story

Found here - http://ImmortalityBooks.com

Other books by this author: http://MichaelMathiesen.com

www.ingramcontent.com/pod-product-compliance
Lightning Source LLC
Chambersburg PA
CBHW071157050326

40689CB00011B/2149